T0360452

Power, Politics and Exclusion in Organization and Management

There is a long tradition of research on politics, power and exclusion in areas such as sociology, social policy, politics, women's studies and philosophy. While power has received considerable attention in mainstream management research and teaching, it is rarely considered in terms of politics and exclusion, particularly where the work of women writers is concerned.

This second book in the Routledge Series on Women Writers in Organization Studies analyses the ways in which women have theorised and embodied relations of power. Women like Edith Garrud who, trained in the Japanese art of jujutsu, confronted the power of the state to champion feminist politics. Others, such as Beatrice Webb and Alva Myrdal, are shown to have been at the heart of welfare reforms and social justice movements that responded to the worst excesses of industrialisation based on considerations of class and gender. The writing of bell hooks provides a necessarily uncomfortable account of the ways in which imperialism, white supremacy and patriarchy inflict unspoken harm, while Hannah Arendt's work considers the ways in which different modes of organizing restrict the ability of people to live freely. Taken together, such writings dispel the myth that work or business can be separated from the rest of life, a point driven home by Rosabeth Moss Kanter's observations on the ways in which power and inequality differentially structure life chances. These writers challenge us to think again about power, politics and exclusion in organizational contexts. They provide provocative thinking, which opens up new avenues for organization theory, practice and social activism.

Each woman writer is introduced and analysed by experts in organization studies. Further reading and accessible resources are also identified for those interested in knowing (thinking!) more. This book will be relevant to students, researchers and practitioners with an interest in business and management, organizational studies, critical management studies, gender studies and sociology. Like all the books in this series, it will also be interest to anyone who wants to see, think and act differently.

Robert McMurray is Professor of Work and Organization at The York Management School, UK. His research interests include the organization of health care, professions, emotion labour, dirty work and visual methods. Other collaborative book projects include *The Dark Side of Emotional Labour* (2015), *The Management of Wicked Problems in Health and Social Care* (2018) and *Urban Portraits* (2017).

Alison Pullen is Professor of Management and Organization Studies at Macquarie University, Australia and Editor-in-Chief of *Gender, Work and Organization*. Alison's research has been concerned with analysing and intervening in the politics of work as it concerns gender discrimination, identity politics and organizational injustice.

Routledge Focus on Women Writers in Organization Studies

Given that women and men have always engaged in and thought about organizing, why is it that core management texts are dominated by the writing of men? This series redresses the neglect of women in organization thought and practice and highlights their contributions. Through a selection of carefully curated short-form books, it covers major themes such as structure, rationality, managing, leading, culture, power, ethics, diversity and sustainability; and also attends to contemporary debates surrounding performativity, the body, emotion, materiality and post-coloniality. Individually, each book provides stand-alone coverage of a key sub-area within organization studies, with a contextual series introduction written by the editors. Collectively, the titles in the series give a global overview of how women have shaped organizational thought.

Routledge Focus on Women Writers in Organization Studies will be relevant to students and researchers across business and management, organizational studies, critical management studies, gender studies and sociology. *Edited by Robert McMurray and Alison Pullen*

Beyond Rationality in Organization and Management
Edited by Robert McMurray and Alison Pullen

Power, Politics and Exclusion in Organization and Management
Edited by Robert McMurray and Alison Pullen

For more information about this series, please visit: www.routledge.com/ Routledge-Focus-on-Women-Writers-in-Organization-Studies/book-series/ RFWWOS

Power, Politics and Exclusion in Organization and Management

Edited by
Robert McMurray and Alison Pullen

Routledge
Taylor & Francis Group

LONDON AND NEW YORK

First published 2019
by Routledge
2 Park Square, Milton Park, Abingdon, Oxon OX14 4RN

and by Routledge
52 Vanderbilt Avenue, New York, NY 10017

Routledge is an imprint of the Taylor & Francis Group, an informa business

British Library Cataloguing-in-Publication Data
A catalogue record for this book is available from the British Library

Library of Congress Cataloging-in-Publication Data
A catalog record has been requested for this book

ISBN: 978-0-367-23399-0 (hbk)
ISBN: 978-0-429-27968-3 (ebk)

Typeset in Times New Roman
by Deanta Global Publishing Services, Chennai, India

Contents

Series note

This series arose from the question: given that women and men have always engaged in, and thought about, organizing, why are core management texts dominated by the writing of men? Relatedly, and centrally to the development of organization studies as a field, the following questions become central: why do so few women theorists and writers appear in our lectures and classes on managing, organizing and working? Why have the contributions of women to organization theory been neglected and, indeed, written out of the everyday conversations of the academy?

This series redresses the neglect of women in organization thought and practice. It does so by highlighting the unique contributions of women in respect to fundamental organizational issues such as structure, rationality, managing, leading, culture, power, ethics, diversity and sustainability, while also attending to more nuanced organizational concerns arising from issues such as performativity, the body, emotion, materiality and post-coloniality.

Through a selection of carefully curated short-form books, the series provides an overview of how women have shaped organizational thought. It is international in scope, drawing on ideas, concepts, experiences and writing from across Europe, North America and Australasia, and spanning more than 150 years. As the series develops, our ambition is to move beyond even these confines to encompass the work of women from all parts of the globe.

This is not a standard textbook. It does not offer a chronological history of women in organization theory. It does not (cannot) claim to be the complete or the last word on women in organization: the contribution of women to organization theory and practice continues and grows. We do not even promise that each chapter will be written like the one that preceded it! Why? It is because the variation in style and substance of each chapter deliberately reflects the varied, exciting and often transgressive women discussed. Indeed, one of the points of this series is to draw attention to the possibility that there are as many ways of thinking about, writing on and doing organizing as there are people. If you want to read and think differently about management work and organization, then this is the series for you.

Readers of this and other volumes in the series will note that the first person is often employed in our accounts of women writers. Reference is made to meetings with writers, to the personal impact of their thinking and to the ways in which writers have moved or challenged their researchers personally. Once again, this personal emotional approach to assessing the work of others is at odds with more positivistic or masculine approaches that contend that the researcher or analyst of organizations is to remain outside, beyond or above the subject matter: an expert eye whose authorial tone allows them to act as dispassionate judge on the work of others. We argue that the fallacy of neutrality that results from such masculine positivism hides the arbitrary and inherently bias nature of subject selection, appraisal and writing. Just as importantly, it tends to produce sterile prose that does little to convey the excitement and dynamism of the ideas being discussed.

The subject matter of this book has been chosen because the chapter creators believe it to be important, and particular thought has been given to the selection of the women writers shared with you. Authors recognise the bias inherent in any writing project; it is writ large in the title of the series (Focus on Women Writers) and is more explicit in some chapters than in others. In editing this series, we have been struck with the enthusiasm that informs how our authors have chosen influential women writers, and this enthusiasm can be read in the ways in which the chapters engage with the work of specific writers, in the application of these writers to organization studies and in the personal reflections on the influence of these writers on the authors' own research. The perspective from which we – and our authors – write is therefore open for you (the reader) to read, acknowledge and account for in the multiple ways intended. The lack of consistency with which the authors address fundamental organizational issues should not be read as lacking rigour, but rather bring an alternative way of leveraging critical thinking through an engaged, personal approach to the field. In this way, authors embody the ideas and ethos of the women writers chosen. While written in an accessible form, each chapter is based on years of engagement with the works of particular writers and an in-depth appreciation of their contribution to and impact on organization studies. There is also critique. The omissions or controversies that have accompanied the work of particular writers are addressed, along with challenges to their work.

The result is a collection of books on women writers that are scholarly, readable and engaging. They introduce you to some of the most important concepts in organization studies from some of the best theorists in the field. Politically and ethically, we hope that this book will help students, lecturers and practitioners reverse a trend that has seen women writers written out of organization theory. Just as importantly, the inclusion of such work usefully challenges many long-held beliefs within mainstream management literature. We hope that this series will be the beginning of your own personal journey of ideas – the text and suggested readings produced in this book offering a starting point for your own discoveries.

The Routledge Focus on Women Writers in Organization Studies series will be relevant to students, teachers and researchers across business and management, organizational studies, critical management studies, gender studies and sociology.

Robert McMurray and Alison Pullen

Contributors

Peter Bloom is a Senior Lecturer and Head of the Department of People and Organizations at the Open University, Co-Founder of the research group REEF (Research into Employment, Empowerment and Futures). His books include *Authoritarian Capitalism in the Age of Globalization* (2016), *Beyond Power and Resistance: Politics at the Radical Limits* (2016), *The Ethics of Neoliberalism: The Business of Making Capitalism Moral* (2017), *The Bad Faith in the Free Market: The Radical Promise of Existential Freedom* (2018) and *CEO Society: The Corporate Takeover of Everyday Life*, (2018) co-written with Carl Rhodes. His scholarly work has also been published in leading international journals and informed global media outlets.

The Open University Business School, Open University, UK.

peter.bloom@open.ac.uk

Deborah Brewis is a Lecturer in Organization Studies at the University of Bath School of Management, UK. Her research examines the concepts, practices and politics with which we organize "difference" in and around work. Specifically, gender and race in working life, inclusion/exclusion in digital work, affect and emotions surrounding change and solidarity work. She is involved in writing differently about management and organization and in promoting anti-racist practice in higher education.

School of Management, University of Bath, UK.

D.brewis@bath.ac.uk

David Jacobs is an Associate Professor of Labour and Sustainability at the Graves School of Business at Morgan State University in Baltimore, Maryland. His teaching and research are informed by the concept of social invention and the application of imagination to the design of social institutions. David has published articles in *Academy of Management Learning and Education*, the *Academy of Management Review*, *Ephemera*, *Labor Studies Journal*, *Negotiation Journal*, *Perspectives on Work* and other refereed outlets. He is the author or editor of five books, including *The Future of the Safety Net* (2001) and *The Internet, Organizational Change, and Labour* (2003).

Graves School of Business, Morgan State University, USA.

david.jacobs@Morgan.edu

Simon Kelly is a Senior Lecturer in Management at the University of Huddersfield Business School, UK. Simon's research is concerned with critical and alternative approaches to leadership, followership, ethics, embodiment and organization. His research has been published in international journals including *Human Relations*, *Journal of Business Ethics*, *Leadership* and *Organization*.

Department of Management, The Business School, University of Huddersfield, UK.

s.kelly@hud.ac.uk

Helena Liu is a Senior Lecturer at UTS Business School in Sydney, Australia. Central to her research is the critique of how gender, racial and class dynamics sustain our enduring romance with leadership. Helena is currently writing her first book with Bristol University Press on anti-racist feminist movements and how they may help us rethink leadership theorising and practice.

UTS Business School, University of Technology Sydney, Australia.

helena.liu@uts.edu.au

Robert McMurray is a Professor of Work and Organization at The York Management School, UK. His research interests include the organization of health care, professions, emotion labour, dirty work and visual methods. Other collaborative book projects include *The Dark Side of Emotional*

Labour (2015), *The Management of Wicked Problems in Health and Social Care* (2018) and *Urban Portraits* (2017).

The York Management School, University of York, UK.

Robert.mcmurray@york.ac.uk

Rosetta Morris has taught at the University of Phoenix and Morgan State University. Her research focuses on contradictory currents in the discipline of human resource management. She has presented papers in symposia at the Academy of Management and published in the *Journal of Management History*, among other academic outlets. Rosetta has been a Galbraith Fellow at the Americans for Democratic Action Education Fund.

morrisra7@gmail.com

Lara Pecis is a Lecturer in Organization Studies at Lancaster University Management School, UK. Lara's research interests include issues of marginalisation and inclusion at work, in particular in innovation-intensive contexts, and in relation to the politics of technologies.

Department of Organization, Work and Technology, Lancaster University Management School, UK.

l.pecis@lancaster.ac.uk

Alison Pullen is a Professor of Management and Organization Studies at Macquarie University, Australia and Editor-in-Chief of *Gender, Work and Organization*. Alison's research has been concerned with analysing and intervening in the politics of work as it concerns gender discrimination, identity politics and organizational injustice.

Department of Management, Macquarie University, Austalia.

Alison.pullen@mq.edu.au

Torkild Thanem is a Professor of Management and Organization Studies at Stockholm Business School, Stockholm University, Sweden. He is an Associate Editor of the journal *Organization* and a former Associate Editor of *Gender, Work & Organization* (2009–2018). Torkild currently pursues two lines of research: a project studying fitness and wellness in corporate performance cultures, and a project focusing on the lived practices, experiences and politics of trans people. His most recent work has been published in *Business Ethics Quarterly, Harvard Business Review* and *Organization*. His forthcoming book (co-authored with David Knights) is titled *Embodied Research Methods* and will be published in 2019.

Stockholm Business School, Stockholm University, Sweden.

tt@sbs.su.se

Louise Wallenberg is an Associate Professor in Fashion Studies and former Director of the Centre for Fashion Studies at Stockholm University. Her publications include the co-edited volumes *Fashion and Modernism* (2018); *Fashion, Film and the 1960s* (2018); *Harry bit för bit* (2017); *Modernism och mode* (2014); *Nordic Fashion Studies* (2011) and *MODE* (2009).

Section for Fashion Studies at the Department of Media Studies at Stockholm University, Sweden.

louise@fashion.su.se

1 Introduction

Power, politics and exclusion

Robert McMurray and Alison Pullen

Power and politics are an inescapable part of organizing. Organizations are political arenas infused by power, where authority and influence reside in the ways in which relationships are negotiated and formed. There can be no action in the absence of relations of power, and decisions and negotiations cannot be divorced from the play of politics in so far as resources and vested interests are always in play as stakeholders vie for supremacy. Drawing on psychology, sociology, politics, philosophy and history, our understanding of power in organization and management has become more nuanced. Unitary assumptions have been challenged by accounts of pluralistic interests, politics and non-decision-making power. Simplistic trait-based notions of individual power have been found wanting in the face of more relational accounts that stress the inter-relational spaces between people. Moreover, power is increasingly read as embedded within and reproduced by deep structures and discrete processes that both constitute and are constituted by interacting agents. This combination of actors, structures and processes produces an uneven distribution of opportunities, resources and outcomes. The evidence of these power relations is writ large in everything, from stories of heroic business leaders to the everyday coercion of unseen workers, to the accounts of sexual harassment at work and the aggregated demands of consumers.

Given the wealth of writings on "power", one might question why the topic is tackled in this series on Women Writers in Organization Studies. Most literature on power assumes gender neutrality (Wilson, 1996), yet all too often accounts of power are written by men about men's lives, and as such scholars of organization adopt gender-blind perspectives. Whether the focus is CEOs, industrial relations, labour process theory, change management, mergers and acquisitions or business history, there is a tendency to focus on the lives, experiences or theorising of men. While this is not always the case, it is fair to say that the experience and theorising of women is, taken as a whole, underrepresented. Where women are present in the analysis of their organizational lives, the focus tends to be on their representation – that is to say they are counted to determine how many women are in the organization. Much of the literature focuses on their relative subordination to men in male-dominated organizations. Consequently, many of us are blind to what it has meant, and continues to mean, to work, manage, lead and organize as women given that organizational textbooks continue to represent the lives of the neutral worker, manager and executive as default male. As importantly, not enough is read about alternative conceptualisations of the nature of work, organization and management – conceptions rooted in the theorising and experiences of women. This includes the ways in which women have organized to oppose their exclusion and assert their right to shape the world. Further, there is a growing body of feminist studies of organizations that explore feminist ways of organizing, thinking and writing.

Building on *Beyond Rationality in Organization and Management*, Volume 1 of the Routledge Focus on Women Writers in Organization Studies series, this volume considers the ways in which women have created their own positions from which to challenge the power, politics and exclusion. In so doing, Volume 2 considers the life of Edith Garrud (trained in the Japanese art of jujutsu) who confronted the power of others in a literal and conceptual sense to champion feminist politics as a counterpoint to classical management thinking. Others, such as Beatrice Webb and Alva Myrdal, are shown to have been at the heart of welfare reforms and social-justice movements that responded to the worst excesses of industrialisation, bringing particular attention to issues of gender and class. Such writing has the benefit of dispelling the myth that work or business can be separated from the rest of life, a point driven home by the work of Rosabeth Moss Kanter, a writer who considered power and inequality in the light of work–family dynamics. The scholarship of Hannah Arendt provides a sustained critique of sovereign power and how to challenge and transcend traditional and patriarchal forms of governance linked to values of control. Finally, and importantly, the writing and activism of bell hooks reminds us that issues of power, politics and exclusion are not only about class and gender, but also about race. Together, these writers challenge us to think again about power, politics and exclusion in organizational contexts. They open new avenues for organization theory and practice and social activism.

Given that this book is published 100 years after the granting of votes for (some) women in Britain, it is appropriate that we begin the volume with an account of the struggle, violence and opposition that shaped the suffragette movement. Reaching back to the late 19th and early 20th century, Simon Kelly describes the extraordinary life of a woman who wrote a limited amount, but nonetheless embodied a very particular and disruptive form of organizing and acting that fundamentally challenged the status quo: Edith Garrud. The status quo was represented by politicians and poets such as Ruskin, who lionised the apparent physicality, force, progressiveness and conquering abilities of men, while describing women as frail, beautiful, marginal, lacking in creativity yet capable of praising the achievements of men. In short, a woman was less than a man. Edith Garrud is described as resisting such positioning in cultural, political and legal terms. An expert in jujutsu, defender of the suffragettes, performer and political activist, Garrud co-opts the male art of fighting to construct women and women's bodies as active, threatening and powerful in the face of male dominance. As Simon Kelly notes, rather than being seen as passive and possessable, women's bodies become spaces for the practice of politics, resistance, identity and change. Edith Garrud trained women in the self-defence required to claim public space, while also offering suffragettes the physical means to counter the agents of an oppressive tate (not to mention casual and institutional sexual abuse). This then, is a story of heroic feminism capable of organizing and claiming space in the face of male/masculine opposition. It points to the possibility of resisting marginal positions and the different ways in which strength might be embodied and employed. This is not a chapter about organizing and managing per se. Rather, it invites us to reconsider how our everyday assumptions might marginalise and oppress those with whom we work, while highlighting the potential for the oppressed to oppose such action.

Where Edith Garrud can be characterised as a self-made publicist and business owner, Beatrice Webb has a rather different societal position. David Jacobs and Rosetta Morris' Chapter 3 makes clear that Webb's personal life of wealth and privilege was in stark contrast to her concern with equality and advancement. Spanning the roles of society hostess, charity worker, social scientist and social reformer, Beatrice eschewed mainstream concerns with elites and professions (a concern that persists today) in favour of understanding the structural conditions that maintain disadvantage and poverty. As with other writers in this series (see, for example, Kenny [Forthcoming] on Berlant), Beatrice Webb dared to look differently at work, often from the perspective of those at the bottom of society. While Webb was no radical, we learn that she was prepared to challenge extant theory, particularly neoclassical economics, based on first-hand observation and data collection. Beatrice Webb recognised that organizing, politics, power and justice are not distinct academic subjects but, rather, the intertwined processes embedded in social systems that maintain conditions of relative disadvantage. It is not surprising then that Beatrice Webb contributed to our understanding of economics, productive wages, welfare and political reform. Moreover, she employed her research and writing to actively campaign for the improvement of living conditions in each of these areas. Given that Beatrice Webb was acutely aware of the conditions that maintain disadvantage, it is ironic that those forces would see her marginalised – her full contribution written out of an arena dominated by men. Specifically, David and Rosetta say that Beatrice Webb was required to step down as the literary executor to British philosopher and sociologist Herbert Spencer. The cause? Her marriage to Sidney Webb, a man with whose politics Spencer disagreed. Spencer felt that Beatrice's association with Sidney would embarrass him. In response, Beatrice agreed to assist Spencer without ever being acknowledged. This rather prosaic point goes to the heart of how women's work is often unacknowledged in, and written out of, academic labour and history. It reminds us of why chapters such as this are so important and calls for a corrective to histories and texts that are partial and exclusionary. We are all the poorer for such acts of exclusion.

It is unusual that Chapter 4 should introduce the work of a person who combines feminism and eugenic social engineering, but this is precisely what is on offer when Louise Wallenberg and Torkild Thanem consider Swedish politician and intellectual Alva Myrdal. Like many of the women in this series, Alva Myrdal's life and work has been either under-recognised or forgotten. We learn that underpinning Myrdal's politics was a relentless striving to create a classless society where women and men were treated as equals. Equality was to be based on the premise that a person's abilities were a question of nurture – predicated on social and economic conditions – rather than nature. This was taken to imply a strong role of the welfare state if women were to fulfil their wider potential unfettered by the unequal distribution of domestic labour. Louise and Torkild describe Alva's fight against the patriarchal construction of what she regarded as a "fake femininity" – which oppressed and subordinated women by reducing them to "mothers and wives" – a fully 20 years before Simone de Beauvoir articulated very similar ideas in *The Second Sex*. The result is a politics which positions the State as a central player in the transformation of work, organizing and business. Alva also fundamentally challenged essentialist conceptions of the role of women in Sweden. For many readers, the link to social eugenics in Alva Myrdal's work will be rightly problematic. Even allowing for context, its fascist overtones speak to potential intolerance of difference, promoting as they do a concern with "efficient" human capital in its most unpalatable form. While such a position is framed in terms of the interests of society as a whole, it reflects a sentiment at odds with our understanding of the role of a compassionate welfare state. Indeed, as Louise Wallenberg and Torkild Thanem note, the Swedish government has latterly offered economic compensation to victims of Sweden's coercive sterilisation scheme. And yet, Alva Myrdal was a Nobel Peace Prize winner and director of UNESCO who fundamentally challenged existing power structures. What this account of Alva Myrdal reminds us of is that ideas and the people who create them are complex, contextually bound and contestable. Like all writers, the authors studied in this book are not to be taken at their word, but are to be critically examined to determine the areas in which their thinking is to be judged wanting, but also those where their writing might enlighten our understanding of self in relation to other. In this sense, our writers mirror the complexity of the wider world and the power and politics that mark its course.

In Chapter 5, we move forward to the present day and cross continents to the USA. Deborah N. Brewis and Lara Pecis introduce Rosabeth Moss Kanter: an influential scholar and practitioner whose writing has contributed to our understanding of infrastructure, power, leadership, regeneration, gender, diversity, innovation and change. Recognising that a single chapter cannot hope to cover such a breadth of contribution, Deborah and Lara prioritise the contributions of two of Kanter's books. The first, *Men and Women of the Corporation*, is presented as a nuanced account of the gendering of the formal and informal roles that shape the work of organizational actors and contribute to corporate functioning. Relational in outlook, Rosabeth Moss Kanter's research is praised for considering how the structuring of roles, relations, hierarchies, practices and power not only determines but positively or negatively reinforces the life chances of different individuals. Particular attention is paid to the ways in which women, as a minority, suffer marginalisation and tokenism as a consequence of the over-representation of men and masculinity in our organizations. Here, Kanter refers to the repressive and self-regulating effects of the male gaze (as pertinent an issue now as it was in the 1970s) that categorises and entraps minorities in general and women in particular. Having considered the significance of Kanter's contribution in this area, Deborah N. Brewis and Lara Pecis go on to consider how her works have been extended in respect of leadership, gender, embodiment and the fallacy of organizational neutrality. The latter part of the chapter considers Kanter's contribution to our understanding of change and innovation arising out of the book *The Change Masters: Innovations for Productivity in the American Corporation*. The resulting analysis usefully extends our understanding of empowerment in organization studies and provides an account of innovation that foreshadows and informs research in organizational studies for decades to come.

Peter Bloom rightly describes Hannah Arendt as one of the foremost intellectuals of the 20th century. Having outlined the broad sweep and significance of Hannah Arendt's writing, Peter focuses attention on the ways in which her work illuminates our understanding of power and organizing. Chapter 6 presents a range of concepts through which Arendt interrogates our ways of being in the world (e.g. labour, work, action, vita activa organizing, the human condition, worldly alienation and vita management). Writing at a time of global upheaval and threat, Hannah Arendt is concerned with the ways in which politics and organizing restrict the ability of people to freely organize their work, life and actions. Rationality, probability, regulation, institutionalisation and quantification serve to limit space for individuality and difference as we are imprisoned by industrialisation, capitalism and marketisation. For Hannah Arendt, such limitations are not to be seen as an inevitable consequence of inviolable behavioral or institutional laws, but rather, as discursive accomplishments whose existence depends on practices of legitimation. The chapter leads us to question the power of late capitalism to define and limit us as human beings. As Peter Bloom notes, the challenge becomes one of conceiving modes of organizing that meet basic needs while promoting the individual freedom required to meaningfully create, relate and live.

Our exploration of power, politics and exclusion is brought to a close by Helena Liu's powerful account of bell hooks. Traversing the boundary between academic theorising and public intellectualism over the last four decades, bell hooks' extensive library has offered a bold, plainspoken critique of the hegemonic culture of violence in our societies. hooks' writings engage in a politics of decolonisation, disrupting our internalisation of the dominant values embedded in what she poignantly calls "the imperialist white supremacist capitalist patriarchy". Over more than thirty books, bell hooks has developed a vocabulary for naming what often remains unspoken. In particular, her work allows us to disrupt the silences in management-theorising and practice and challenge the ways we reproduce, if not glorify, systems of imperialism, white supremacy, capitalism and patriarchy. hooks' writing may prove uncomfortable reading for many, as it attacks the tokenistic self-interest of men who promote parity while leaving marginalising structures and patriarchal practices in place. Feminism is similarly critiqued in so far as it fails to account for race and lacks the radical thought required to engender fundamental change. bell hooks reminds us that the point of theorising and organizing is action. Helena Liu notes that, to date, such radical theorising and action have been conspicuous by their absence in management and organization studies. Patriarchy and white supremacy have for too long been unspeakable: silenced issues within the academy, workplace and society. The first step is to acknowledge the exclusion (and exclusionary effects) of these topics, coupled with a radical visionary feminist politics that has a non-dominating love at its root.

Taken together, the books in this volume encourage us to look again at the nature and effects of power on individuals, groups, organizations and society. They demonstrate the ways in which power and politics combine to marginalise, exclude and erase some whilst serving the interests of others. Further, these books bring to the surface the different ways in which power and exclusionary practices have, can and should be opposed for the benefit of all. Writing, and writing to educate, is a powerful practice which needs to be followed up by action.

References

Kenny, K. (Forthcoming). Lauren Berlant: Cruel organizations. In McMurray, R. and Pullen, A. (Eds.), *Morality, Ethics and Responsibility, Organization and Management, Routledge Focus on Women Writers in Organization Studies.* London: Routledge.

Wilson, F. (1996). Research note: Organizational theory: Blind and deaf to gender? *Organization Studies*, 17(5), pp. 825–842.

2   Edith Garrud

The jujutsuffragette

Simon Kelly

The argument against Woman Suffrage which has always impressed me most is the physical force argument. First, the only stable force of government is the one which secures that the balance of political power is in the same hands as the balance of physical force. Second, by counting heads you secure a rough approximate index as to where government or policy has the physical force of the country behind it. In the last place, women as physical force units are not equal to men. Therefore, if you include women when you are counting heads, the result is not reliable as an index of the physical force in the country.

Alexander MacCallum Scott, Liberal MP
for Glasgow Bridgeton[1]

The words above epitomise the political struggle and symbolic challenges facing women fighting for the right to vote in Britain during the early years of the 20th century. The extract above is taken from a longer parliamentary transcript of debates surrounding the introduction of a bill that would allow a select group of property-owning women the right to vote. This was the third Conciliation Bill to be put before the Houses of Parliament with previous bills either failing to be heard or being withdrawn due to lack of votes. This third and final bill suffered the same fate as its predecessors and it wasn't until 1918 that a select group of women and men in the UK were granted the right to vote. MacCallum Scott's contribution to this debate captures perfectly the justifications made for preventing women from voting. Back then, as today, the final card to be played in such debates about gender equality often draws on a particular notion of *strength*. One gender, we are told, has strength; the other lacks it. Moreover, we are told that physical strength can and should be equated to political power as only those physically able to defend and protect the borders and interests of a sovereign State should have a say in the political life of a nation and how it should be governed. In making a contribution to women writers in organization studies, this chapter introduces a woman who lived during the Conciliation Bill debates and who experienced and also helped to shape some of the events surrounding the Votes for Women movement. In her own unique way, she directly challenged such assumptions about strength to reveal an alternative notion of embodied physical and political power. Yet the woman discussed here, named Edith Margaret Garrud, is unusual in this book series in that she has not directly contributed to the academic study of organizations and management. Neither is she a renowned philosopher or social thinker. Her writings are generally quite sparse, and we know very little of her early years or later life. However, Edith Garrud as a person, a body, a writer, a suffragette, a martial arts instructor, performer and choreographer, has a significant contribution to make for an understanding of organizing and organization – and particularly for an appreciation of gender equality, power, politics and exclusion.

Born Edith Margaret Williams in Bath, Somerset, UK in 1872, Edith Garrud was a physical culture instructor, suffragette, and one of Great Britain's leading martial arts practitioners of the early 20th century. Her martial arts specialism was the Japanese art of *jujutsu*[2]: an art that specialises in speed, precision and the use of soft flowing movements to absorb, disrupt and redirect force and aggression rather than seeking to oppose them with brute strength. Translated crudely from its original Japanese, the term jujutsu itself means the "gentle art of yielding" and was cultivated by the Samurai class in feudal Japan as a form of unarmed battlefield combat (Wingard, 2003). Edith Garrud and her husband William became early adopters, expert practitioners and instructors in this esoteric late-Victorian form of fighting art as it travelled from its origins in East Asia to Western Europe in the late 1800s. Already a renowned martial arts performer and instructor, Edith was later approached by Emmeline Pankhurst to train members of the Women's Social and Political Union (WSPU) and eventually became the leader of the athletics branch of the Women's Freedom League (WFL) and chief instructor of The Bodyguard – a secret group of highly trained suffragette activists appointed as agitators and protectors of the WSPU inner circle and its leaders. In her role as jujutsu practitioner and suffragette, Edith was a vocal campaigner for the Votes for Women movement and used her position and reputation as a skilled martial artist to challenge popular views and assumptions about the place of women in society. In her writings, through her instruction and in public performances, Edith provided women and men with a new understanding of what strong femininity might look like and how women might use bodily practices such as jujutsu to challenge and (in some cases quite literally) overturn a patriarchal organizational order in which political power and status were, and arguably still are, equated with narrow and misleading notions of masculine physical strength and muscular domination.

Co-opting the gentlemanly art of fighting

> The man's power is active, progressive, defensive. He is eminently the doer, the creator, the discoverer, the defender [...] But the woman's power is for rule, not for battle – and her intellect is not for invention or creation, but for sweet ordering [...] she enters into no contest, but infallibly adjudges the crown of contest.
>
> John Ruskin, "Of Queens' Gardens" (1865: 99)

The world into which Edith Garrud was born was one where the writings of poets such as John Ruskin provided the aesthetic and cultural landscape and social framework for how each gender should be defined and how their capabilities and actions might be properly evaluated and chartered over one's life course. His romantic vision of the sexes expressed in his essay "Of Queens' Gardens" published in 1865, just seven years before Edith's birth, set out a powerful masculinised vision of the nature of woman – at least "woman" in John Ruskin's imagination and that of the late Victorian establishment. Women and their bodies were to be considered pure, untainted, beautiful, but also passive, decorative and delicate. More importantly, they should recognise their place in the world as praise givers and domestic decision-makers. They should not engage in contests, but instead watch with admiration from the sidelines. Where prominent public figures such as Ruskin traced out the cultural and social norms for the feminine and the masculine, the late-19th-century British legal and political systems also provided the rigid structures by which men and women must be governed and through which they should organize their lives and their labours according to gendered expectations. If follows, then, that those not suited to contest and the demands of warfare or to the challenges of creativity, cannot be given power to determine good governance. Yet this lack of political status would not prevent women and their bodies from being subjects of government (Crawford, 1999; Pankhurst, 1931). This is attested to in an array of laws and customs which governed the lives and in particular the bodies of late- 19th- and early 20th-century women, such as the Criminal Conversation action, in which a husband could sue his wife's lover for trespassing on his property. The act was repealed in 1857 but was accompanied by many others, including the Contagious Diseases Act of 1864–1869 in which women (and specifically sex workers) could be prosecuted, fined and even forcibly committed to secure "lock hospitals" if it was suspected that they suffered from sexually transmitted diseases (Mendus and Rendall, 1989). The reason for this harsh penalty was that, aside from the infected female sex workers, the other group most affected were members of the British armed forces. Here again, we have echoes of the same arguments laid out earlier by MacCallum Scott and Ruskin: that men, as the doers, the defenders and the creative discoverers, must be protected from the excesses, threats and debilitations caused by encounters with femininity. Women of the 19th century were therefore required to adhere to the Ruskinian vision of the passive, pure and delicate lady, or risk being cast out as the active, dirty, abject and infectious seductress.

It was against this backdrop of gendered expectations, and only three years following the repeal of the controversial Contagious Diseases Act, that Edith Margaret Williams was born in 1872 in the English county of Somerset. Edith was raised in Wales and educated in England where she trained as a school teacher specialising in physical culture instruction for girls.[3] It was through this shared passion for physical culture that Edith met her husband William Garrud – a fellow instructor specialising in boxing and wrestling. Together they moved to London, where the public fascination with and demand for physical culture instruction was as its peak at the turn of the century. According to Wolf (2009), in 1900, Edith and William read about an evening performance at the Alhambra Theatre in London by the then-famous Mr Edward William Barton-Wright, who would be demonstrating a novel form of wrestling.[4] Such performances of physical culture and prize fighting were already popular as forms of music hall entertainment. For figures such as Barton-Wright, this was also an opportunity to market jujutsu to an English audience and so promote his newly established Bartitsu School of Arms and Physical Culture. As was typical during such performances, Barton-Wright stood on stage wearing the traditional white Japanese training *gi* and invited members of the public to try to attack him. Using jujutsu grappling techniques, sweeps and joint locks he was able to control and disable each opponent without harming them. When performing each move, Barton-Wright also provided a commentary to the audience in which he emphasised that jujutsu was unlike boxing and wrestling in that it was more than a sport – it was an art form, a type of bodily expression with self-defence as its purpose (Barton-Wright, 1899; Wolf, 2005). Impressed with Barton-Wright's demonstration, Edith and William took up the invitation to study this new fighting art and became students of Bartitsu under Barton-Wright's instruction.

By 1902, the Bartitsu Club had closed due to declining membership, with Barton-Wright pursuing an interest in physical therapy techniques and leaving his chief instructors Yukio Tani and Sadakazu Uyenishi to continue their own traditional Japanese jujutsu classes at a new training room or *dojo* in nearby Golden Square on Oxford Street, London (Godfrey, 2010; Wolf, 2005). Having already become proficient in jujutsu themselves, Edith and William Garrud continued training with Tani and Uyenishi and an array of visiting prominent Japanese jujutsu masters at the Golden Square School from 1902 until 1908. When eventually Tani and Uyenishi decided to return to Japan, they left the club under the ownership of their now-assistant instructors William and Edith. From this point the couple took over instruction of jujutsu themselves, with William continuing to instruct the men's classes and Edith establishing new classes for women and children. This shift from student to instructor allowed the Garruds to build their own reputation as jujutsu martial arts specialists in London without the trappings of the Bartitsu brand (Wolf, 2009). The novel inclusion of a female instructor in Edith also coincided with a growing interest among women of the upper classes in physical culture and the self-defence benefits of learning a fighting art from the "mysterious" Far East.[5] Following the example set by their former instructors, the Garruds also took to the stage in music hall exhibitions and public demonstrations to advertise the benefits of jujutsu specifically for women's physical well-being and personal protection. One unique part of the demonstration would include Edith showing the power of jujutsu to overpower a male aggressor as played by William. The scene of a 4ft-11inch female effortlessly throwing a 6ft man over her shoulder and controlling him with some exotic form of wrist or shoulder lock provided onlookers with new possibilities of what a female fighting art might look like, and what a female might be capable of (Looser, 2011). Indeed, Edith's abilities had already attracted the attention of the Pathé film company, who in 1907 employed her as the star of their short film *Ju-jutsu Downs the Footpads*, in which an innocent lady walking the streets of London uses her jujutsu skills to resist and overcome two male ruffians (the titular "footpads"). Designed to showcase this new female martial artist and her skill, this film is also arguably one of the UK's first recognisable martial arts movies, but one that is sadly lost to history with no surviving footage in existence (Godfrey, 2012). Edith and William would continue to run the Golden Square dojo as owners and instructors until their retirement in 1925, when the training hall finally closed. The building itself was later demolished, leaving no trace of its existence. Fortunately, Edith's accomplishments as a martial artist and political activist live on through her lasting contribution to the women's suffrage movement.

The suffragette who knew jujutsu

Edith and William had always taken a keen interest in the growing calls for female political representation, with Edith becoming a member of newly established suffragette organizations such as the WSPU and WLF. In 1908, in recognition of her contribution to the physical culture movement, Edith was appointed head of the WFL athletics branch. Here she began to combine her martial arts training with her political affiliations. She and William followed in the footsteps of their teacher Barton-Wright by holding jujutsu demonstrations and private instruction for WSPU and WFL members. Their demonstrations not only illustrated the potential of jujutsu to control and subdue male aggression, but also created a sense of public spectacle that chimed with the growing political dissatisfaction of the time (Looser 2011). During such demonstrations, Edith's husband William would don a replica police officer's uniform while Edith would dress the part of a suffragette campaigner to demonstrate the effectiveness of jujutsu techniques for resisting the grip of the authorities. This particular demonstration was also later reconstructed in a series of photographs for the magazine *The Sketch* in July 1910, in an article entitled "If You Want to Earn Some Time Throw a Policeman" (Garrud, 1910a), in which Edith (dressed in full lady's Edwardian hat and dress) and her arresting police officer (William) demonstrate how to apply wrist locks and throws, leg locks and arm bars to control and throw a police officer to the floor (see Godfrey, 2012; Wolf, 2009).

By 1909, Edith's instruction of WSPU and WLF members and her politicisation of her martial arts practice had also drawn the attention of the media, beginning with an editorial written for the physical culture periodical *Health and Strength* entitled "Jujutsuffragettes: A New Terror for the London Police". Although written to ridicule the suffrage cause, the article not only gave Garrud and her fellow jujutsu suffragette students a name – "the jujutsuffragettes", but also provided a platform through which to promote a new aesthetic possibility for the political and campaigning female body. This was a new kind of dangerous and threatening body, one that could assert its own authority, force and power to oppose physical domination and perhaps even overthrow the structural and symbolic dictates of the State. As the editorial of the article exclaimed:

> The Suffragettes have taken up the study of jujutsu; they will very soon emerge as expert practitioners in the art, and then, Oh, Robert! You will have to look to your laurels, and your helmet and your tunic to boot [...] We shall see the Prime Minister as he emerges from No.10, Downing Street, seized suddenly and compelled to kneel for mercy, simply because some fair damsel has put a deadly arm-lock upon him. Mr Winston Churchill, strolling peaceably across Parliament Square, will unexpectedly find himself turning a somersault in the air.[6]
>
> Editorial, *Health and Strength* (1909: 421)

As rumours of the jujutsuffragettes spread across London, a second representation of the heroic martial arts campaigner was further impressed upon the public imagination with the publication of a cartoon in *Punch* magazine in July 1910, with the title "The Suffragette Who Knew Jiu-Jitsu:

The Arrest". Here the cartoon depicts an imaginary scene in which an unnamed small female figure (Edith Garrud in all but name) stands in a fighting pose, backed against metal railings and facing down a horde of large male police officers in mid-combat. Several of the police officers are strewn on the ground with others draped over iron railings, presumably in a failed attempt to make an arrest. The remaining police officers look on, faces contorted in fear, as they shrink back from this empowered fighting female. As with the previous editorial, the cartoon in *Punch* was making fun of the suffragettes, but it also raised questions about the power and capability of the police and government to control this new physically and politically dynamic female body.

In May 1909 and in the midst of this growing media attention and State concerns over the new "jujutsuffragettes" (or Mrs Pankhurst's Amazons as they were also known), Edith and William were invited to give a jujutsu demonstration for the WSPU Bazaar at the Prince's Skating Rink, Knightsbridge in London, attended by Emmeline Pankhurst and senior figures of the movement (Crawford, 1999). Shortly before the demonstration began, William was taken ill and so it fell to Edith to conduct the demonstration alone. Dressed in a striking red *gi* and with words of encouragement from Mrs Pankhurst, Edith provided a solo demonstration of and commentary on jujutsu principles and techniques. This demonstration included inviting members of the audience to test her skill including a sceptical male police officer who, having questioned Edith's ability to control his attack, was subjected to a shoulder throw and landed heavily on the makeshift stage mat (Wolf, 2009). By 1910 with the cartoon in *Punch* cementing her reputation as the "suffragette who knows jujutsu" and with the continued support of WFL and WSPU members, Edith had enough regular students to open a second school of Jujutsu at Argyll Place, near Oxford Street in London. Unlike the Golden Square dojo inherited from Barton-Wright, this new training space allowed Edith to offer exclusive public lessons for women and children, whilst also providing "closed-door" specialist street combat training for increasingly embattled WSPU members and fellow suffragette campaigners (Godfrey, 2012).

It was also during 1910, as the fight for women's suffrage intensified, that Edith Garrud wrote a series of short essays in which she explored the political potential of martial arts practice. Two of her articles appeared in *Health and Strength* magazine – a periodical that had only a year before sought to ridicule Garrud. In her first published piece she responds specifically to the editorial of the previous year by observing how the coining of the phrase "jujutsuffragette" had inadvertently given voice to a galvanised and growing community of female martial artist campaigners:

> In proportion as the Suffragettes increase in number and in power, so also do the Jujutsuffragettes (I believe it was *Health and Strength* who first coined that latter phrase). The daily papers, by their witticisms, smart or otherwise, at the expense of the Suffragette who goes in for jujutsu in order that she may foil her supposed natural enemy, the man in blue, has certainly helped to popularise that mode of self-defence we owe to the Japanese amongst our women, whether they clamour for the vote or not.
>
> Edith Garrud (1910b: 284)

In a second article in the same issue titled "Damsel vs Desperado", Edith goes on to present the principles of jujutsu through her own imaginary scene in which a respectable lady is accosted by a ruffian along a quiet country lane. The description is deliberately comical and demonstrates not only the effectiveness of jujutsu concepts and techniques, but also the power of the martial art to liberate the female body from fear and oppression. The victorious "damsel" in this scene is empowered through physical skill, and through this gains power not only over her male aggressors, but also (and perhaps more importantly) over physical and symbolic space – particularly those quiet and rural public places that women were discouraged from exploring without a male chaperone. As Edith asserts:

> You constantly read in the papers reports of dastardly attacks on helpless women by thieves and ruffians. A woman who knows jujutsu, even though she may not be physically strong, even though she may not have even an umbrella or parasol, is not helpless. I know many women personally who have tried the tricks I shall explain to you and come out on top. They have brought great burly cowards nearly twice their size to their feet and made them howl for mercy.
>
> Edith Garrud (1910c: 101)

Cats, mice and bodyguards

The articles published in *Health and Strength* formed the beginnings of Edith Garrud's writing, through which she would develop something of a martial arts manifesto for female liberation through the disciplined practice and application of jujutsu. In a later piece titled "The World we live in: Self-defence" for the suffragette publication *Votes for Women*, Edith provides a vision for female empowerment gained through dedication to the martial arts:

> Whatever the future may have for us, there is no doubt that the average woman is weaker, in muscular strength, than the average man. Yet in modern life it is not actual muscle that tells. Agility, alertness, dexterity, and endurance are usually of more importance, and it is the Japanese fine art of jujutsu or self-defence that has proved more than a match for mere brute force, and is, therefore, not only a good accomplishment, but a necessary safeguard for the woman who has to defend herself through life. I have done my very best to apply Japanese methods to English wants, and I do not think there is any form of attack which cannot be dealt with, nor any opponent who cannot be defeated with surprising ease.
>
> Edith Garrud (1910d: 355)

Yet as Edith presented her martial arts manifesto for "the world we live in", tensions between the suffragette movement and the authorities reached their peak when in July 1910 the first of three Parliamentary Franchise (Women) Bills – or Conciliation Bills – was presented to the House of Commons. Even though the bill was seen as a compromise in that it offered a select group of one million property-owning women the vote, for the suffragette movement it was an important step forward in a long struggle. However, by November the bill was not given time for debate and was indefinitely held back by the then Prime Minister Herbert Asquith – who was fearful that passing such a bill would jeopardise his plans for re-election. In response, on Friday 18th November 1910 a self-appointed "Women's Parliament" of 300 WSPU members – angry at the government's continued stalling and obstruction – marched on the Houses of Parliament to challenge the legitimacy of the government. They were confronted by ranks of police officers armed with batons. Violence immediately broke out across Parliament Square, and the women of the WSPU were subjected to six hours of beatings and arrests. There were reports of widespread sexual abuse by police officers and male bystanders. Two women died during the confrontation, with a third dying days after her arrest and release from prison (Crawford, 1999). During the violence, a photographer for the *Daily Mirror* newspaper famously captured the image of suffragette Ada Wright being assaulted by a police officer. The image showing her body sprawled on the pavement holding her face while the police officer towered over her became front-page news that shocked the nation, shamed the government and created public sympathy for women's suffrage. The image quickly became the symbol for what the WSPU and the media would later call Black Friday.

Edith Garrud was not present at the events of Black Friday, as her growing status as jujutsu instructor for the WSPU made her too valuable to risk arrest at public events (Wolf, 2009). However, in response to the events of Black Friday, WSPU leader Emmeline Pankhurst requested that Edith provide specialist combat training to a select group of women known privately within the WSPU as the Bodyguard. This group of around 30 women led by committed long-term suffragette campaigner Gertrude Harding were tasked with providing personal protection to the WSPU inner circle and to act as agitators, disruptors and decoys to allow key WSPU members to engage in public speeches while avoiding arrest (Wilson, 1998; Wolf, 2009). In her capacity as chief instructor, Edith provided Bodyguard members with specialist training in self-defence and also in the use of homemade concealed weapons such as wooden India clubs and in the fashioning of cardboard body armour (Godfrey, 2012). Drawing on the "yielding" principles of jujutsu, The Bodyguard members were also trained by Edith in novel tactics to distract or disarm police officers. One effective tactic was to use a jujutsu striking technique aimed directly at a police officer's helmet to knock it from his head. As police officers at that time were held personally accountable for the loss of uniform items and would have to pay for their replacement, knocking the hat off was the best means of distracting an officer long enough to escape arrest (Wolf, 2009).

The presence of The Bodyguard was also essential following the introduction of the Prisoners (Temporary Discharge for Ill Health) Act of 1913. Known as the "Cat and Mouse Act", this new government and police tactic sought to avoid publicly embarrassing confrontations such as Black Friday by tasking police (the cats) with the targeting of known suffragette troublemakers (the mice) and engaging in a deliberate cycle of arrest, imprisonment, release and re-arrest. As imprisoned suffragettes would also engage in hunger strike protests, the authorities responded with brutal force-feeding, and so this release and re-arrest "cat and mouse" pursuit left women exhausted and unable to rejoin the movement. To overcome this, one task set for The Bodyguard was to offer personal protection for newly released suffragettes in order to break this cruel cycle. Secret locations including Edith Garrud's own Golden Square and Argyll Street training halls were turned into safe spaces across London for meetings of the movement and for the protection and recuperation of its members. During an interview in 1965 with journalist Godfrey Winn, Edith recounts one such event when she and a group of her jujutsuffragette students took part in the infamous Oxford Street window-smashing protests and describes how they used her nearby training hall as a hideout to escape pursuing police officers (Winn, 1965). Here they used a secret compartment in the floor to hide their street clothes and quickly don their jujutsu jackets to begin training. When the police banged on the door demanding entry, Edith chastised the officers for interrupting her lesson and ordered them off her property.

In 1911, Edith published one of her final pieces on jujutsu in the form of a fight sequence demonstrating the value of jujutsu for combating domestic violence. Edith personally choreographed and trained the actors who played fictional characters Bill and Eliza Borrer in a short photo-story for *Health and Strength* entitled "Jujutsu as a Husband-Tamer: A Suffragette Play with a Moral" (Garrud, 1911). This oddly light-hearted article featured a series of annotated photographs depicting a woman defending herself from her drunken husband using jujutsu techniques. In the story, Bill's drunken advances were met with blocks, throws, wrist locks and choke holds until he gave up and promised to stop drinking and behave himself. Looking beyond the humour in the article and the uncomfortable trivialising of domestic violence that was not uncommon at this time, the article – like so much of Edith Garrud's work – provided a new aesthetic for female empowerment through the physical and symbolic potential of martial arts practice. For Edith, this was a practice that could serve to reclaim power over the female body in both the domestic and public spheres. Indeed, it was this combination of the physical and the symbolic that provided essential tools not just for Edith Garrud, but for the wider suffragette movement, as illustrated in the suffragette march through London celebrating the coronation of King George V in 1911 in which Edith led the procession of the athletics division of the WFL. Here women and men representing the Votes for Women movement wore pure-white clothing with the purple and green sashes of the WSPU, carrying banners, flags and Votes for Women spears, as they marched by the government offices, newspaper companies and gentlemen's clubs that represented the structural powerbase of the London and British establishment.

Sadly, it is here that the archival record of Edith Garrud's achievements, later life and contributions to the suffragette movement come to an end, as Britain entered the Great War of 1914. Shortly before the outbreak of war, public sympathy for women's suffrage had increased following the tragic death of Emily Wilding Davison on 8 June 1913 at the Epsom Derby, when she was struck by a race horse representing King George V. However, within a year the passion for the vote among WSPU members and the need for a trained Bodyguard was slowly subsumed by the threat of war and the need to contribute the defence of a nation (Crawford, 1999). As such, little is known of Edith Garrud's life beyond 1913, and it was not until June 1965, on Edith Garrud's 93rd birthday, that journalist Godfrey Winn, writing for *Woman* magazine, approached Edith for an interview about her life in an article called "Dear Mrs. Garrud – I wish I'd Known You Then …". Here we learn that Edith and William went on to have children and continued to teach jujutsu and gymnastics until, in 1925, they finally closed their dojo training hall at Golden Square to retire to a quieter life. William passed away at the age of 87 in 1960. During the interview, when asked by Winn what her recipe for happiness, health and a long life was, Edith replied:

> Self-discipline. Of course, I had to be extremely disciplined to succeed at jujutsu and hold my own with men [...] but it is the mind which really has control, not only of your muscles and your limbs and how you use them, but also your thoughts, your whole attitude to life and other people.
>
> (Winn, 1965: 25)

Edith Margaret Garrud died in 1971, and in 2012 members of the Garrud family gathered together in Smart Square in London to celebrate her life and to mount an Islington Council People's Plaque to the building that had been her home (see Williams, 2012). The words on the plaque read: "Edith Garrud 1872–1971. The suffragette who knew jiu-jitsu lived here".

Writing Edith Garrud into organization studies

Towards the end of her interview in 1965 with Godfrey Winn, Edith Garrud was asked if she thought of herself as a heroine. She replied: "If I was, I think I must be the last one that's left". At 93 years of age and witnessing the cultural and political changes of the 1960s happening around her, this reply could be viewed as that of someone feeling out of step with the world. Yet it might also speak to a deeper concern that the cultural and sexual revolution that the '60s brought about came at a moral cost. Such a view would have gained sympathy from another woman writer in this Routledge series, Professor Heather Höpfl, who similarly once wrote of the death of heroines in 2010. Here she laments, as Edith perhaps did, the loss of stories of heroic femininity in which virtues, courage and an indomitable spirit of opposition, rather than resistance, are replaced with forms of emancipation that are often all too conditional on and defined, constructed and maintained by male notions of order (Höpfl, 2010: 405). In sharing these brief accounts of the life and achievements of Edith Garrud, it is hoped that this chapter also provides the reader with a story of heroic femininity and opposition in which notions of strength were once reclaimed and repurposed in the fight for political rights, legal recognition and freedom over self and space. Yet unlike the lives of the more prominent leaders of the WSPU, we do not know much about the life of Edith Garrud, so this chapter has had to rely heavily on limited sources drawn from an equally limited historical record made up of newspaper reports, cartoons and magazine articles. In many ways, these limited sources have also created added mystery surrounding Edith and her fellow jujutsuffragettes, a mystery which in recent years has taken on an almost folkloric quality as tales of a secret group of female martial arts fighters have circulated around news and social media (see Williams, 2012; Ruz and Parkinson, 2015), to mark key dates in the 100-year anniversary of the suffragette movement and the landmark Representation of the People Act (1918).

Here the archival traces of Edith Garrud live on in unusual ways, as in the decision by actor Helena Bonham Carter to rename her character "Edith" for the 2014 movie *Suffragette* (Pathé). As Bonham Carter explained in a later interview: "I found out about this character called Edith Garrud, who was 4'11" and taught the suffragettes jiu-jitsu – basically self-defence – against the police. I based a lot of this character on Edith [...] She's a real inspiration and I thought an amazing story; this woman who is literally 5'1" or even 4'11" and could defend herself against these men twice her weight and twice her size" (Bonham Carter, in Weiss, 2015). Similarly, in the recent publication of Wolf and Vieira's 2015 graphic novel series *Suffrajitsu: Mrs. Pankhurst's Amazons*, we have another reimagining of Edith Garrud as super-heroine, as she and her trusted Bodyguard of highly trained jujutsuffragettes not only battle the male political establishment for the right to vote, but also a shadowy masonic-style masculine cult bent on world domination (Wolf and Vieira, 2015). So perhaps it is here, at the intersection between histori-cal fact and fantastical fiction, that Edith Garrud as martial arts practitioner and woman writer can best be appreciated. She never once wrote explicitly about organizations or management, yet her writings and the way in which she was (and continues to be) written about have important lessons for how we might think about the power, politics and ethics of organizing. Indeed, it is a startling act of exclusion in itself that the suffragette movement has – until now – been largely ignored in the academic study of organizations and related fields of management and leadership. This inclusion of Edith Garrud into a history of women writers of organization studies provides a unique space, not only to reflect upon the history of the suffragette move-ment and its relevance for contemporary studies of organization, but also to learn about another forgotten historical narrative: that of an exclusively female-led European martial arts movement (Looser, 2011; Rouse, 2017). A movement that over a century ago sought to reclaim notions of embodi-ment and strength by redefining the principles and practice of physical and political opposition.

Notes

1 Recorded minutes from the debate on the "Conciliation" Bill, 28 March 1912. From Official Report 5th Series Parliamentary Debates: Commons, Vol xxxvi (25 March–12April 1912), columns 615–732.

2 The term "jujutsu" as translated from Japanese to English can be spelled jujutsu, ju-jutsu, jujitsu, ju-jitsu, or jiu-jitsu. The changes in spelling do not in any way denote a difference in the martial art itself and different spellings often depend simply on geography, cultural trends, and historical time periods.

3 The physical culture movement was developed during the 19th century in Europe and North America as a systematised method of training for bodily fitness and strength. A precursor to bodybuilding, it was a movement generally aimed at men and made famous by practitioners such as Eugen Sandow and Charles Atlas (see Chow, 2015).

4 Barton-Wright was a British engineer who, while working in Japan during the late 1800s, had become proficient in jujutsu and sought to export the art to Britain and Europe by taking advantage of the popular fascination with physical culture and the fighting arts. Renamed 'Bartitsu' by Barton-Wright himself, this was promoted as a new hybrid style of street fighting tailored to meet the needs of the English gentleman (see Godfrey, 2010; Wolf, 2005).

5 Something noted in a *Daily Mirror* article from 1904 entitled "Society Women Wrestlers: Ladies' Craze for Japanese Ju-jitsu" (*Daily Mirror*, 4 April 1904).

6 "Oh, Robert!" refers to Robert Peel, former British Home Secretary and Prime Minister who in 1829 founded the London Metropolitan Police Force and is often regarded as the father of modern policing.

Recommended Reading

Interesting text on Edith Garrud

Wolf, Tony (2009). *Edith Garrud: The Suffragette Who Knew Jujutusu*. Raleigh, NC: Lulu Publications.

Key academic text

Looser, Diana (2011). Radical bodies and dangerous ladies: Martial arts and women's performance 1900–1918. *Theatre Research International*, 36(1), pp. 3–19.

Accessible resource

Godfrey, Emelyne (2012). *Femininity, Crime and Self-Defence in Victorian Literature and Society: From Dagger-Fans to Suffragettes*. Basingstoke: Palgrave Macmillan.

References

Barton-Wright, Edward William (March 1899). The new art of self-defence: How a man may defend himself against every form of attack. *Pearson's Magazine*, 7, pp. 268–275.

Chow, B.D.V. (2015). A professional body: Remembering, repeating and working out masculinities in fin-de-siècle physical culture. *Performance Research*, 20(5), pp. 30–41.

Crawford, Elizabeth (1999). *The Women's Suffrage Movement: A Reference Guide 1866–1928*. London: UCL Press.

Editorial (1909). Ju-jutsuffragettes: A new terror for the London police. *Health and Strength*, 6, p. 421.

Garrud, Edith (1910a). If you want to earn some time throw a policeman. *The Sketch*, July, p. 425.

Garrud, Edith (1910b). The ju-jutsu suffragettes: Mrs Garrud replies to her critics. *Health and Strength*, 7, p. 284.

Garrud, Edith (1910c). Damsel vs desperado. *Health and Strength*, 7, pp. 101–102.

Garrud, Edith (1910d). The world we live in: Self-defence. *Votes for Women* newspaper, 4 March, p. 355.

Garrud, Edith (1911). Ju-jutsu as a husband-tamer: A suffragette play with a moral. *Health and Strength*, 8, p. 339.

Godfrey, Emelyne (2010). *Masculinity, Crime and Self-Defence in Victorian Literature*. Basingstoke: Palgrave Macmillan.

Godfrey, Emelyne (2012). *Femininity, Crime and Self-Defence in Victorian Literature and Society: From Dagger-Fans to Suffragettes*. Basingstoke: Palgrave Macmillan.

Höpfl, Heather (2010). The death of the heroine. *Management and Organizational History*, 5(3–4), pp. 395–407.

Looser, Diana (2011). Radical bodies and dangerous ladies: Martial arts and women's performance, 1900–1918. *Theatre Research International*, 36(1), pp. 3–19.

Mendus, S. and Rendall, J. (1989). *Sexuality and Subordination: Interdisciplinary Studies of Gender in the Nineteenth Century*. Routledge: London.

Pankhurst, E.S. (1931). *The Suffragette Movement: An Intimate Account of Persons and Ideals*. London: Longmans.

Rouse, Wendy, L. (2017). *Her Own Hero: Origins of the Women's Self-Defense Movement*. New York: New York University Press.

Ruskin, John (1865) Lecture II: Of queens' gardens. In Epstein Nord, Deborah (2002) (Ed.) *Sesame and Lilies: John Ruskin*. New Haven and London: Yale University Press, pp. 68–93.

Ruz, Camila and Parkinson, Justin (2015). 'Suffrajitsu': How the suffragettes fought back using martial arts. *BBC News Online*, 5 October 2015. Accessed on 19 November 2017: http://www.bbc.co.uk/news/magazine-34425615.

Weiss, Hayley (2015). Helena Bonham Carter, staple of the screen. *Interview Magazine.com*, 24 August 2015. Accessed on 27 October 2017: https://www.int erviewmagazine.com/film/helena-bonham-carter-staple-of-the-screen#_.

Williams, Rachel (June 2012). Edith Garrud: A public vote for the suffragette who taught martial arts. *The Guardian Newspaper Online*. Accessed on 19 November 2017: https://www.theguardian.com/lifeandstyle/2012/jun/25/edith-garrud-suff ragette-martial-arts.

Wilson, Gretchen (1998). *With All Her Might: The Life of Gertrude Harding, Militant Suffragette*. New York: Holmes & Meier.

Wingard, Geoffrey (2003). Sport, industrialism, and the Japanese "gentle way": Judo in late Victorian England. *Journal of Asian Martial Arts*, 12(2), pp. 16–25.

Winn, Godfrey (1965). Dear Mrs. Garrud – I wish I'd known you then …. *Woman Magazine*, 19 June, pp. 22–25.

Wolf, Tony (Ed.) (2005). *The Bartitsu Compendium*. Morrisville, NC: Lulu Publications.

Wolf, Tony (2009). *Edith Garrud: The Suffragette Who Knew Jujutusu*. Raleigh, NC: Lulu Publications.

Wolf, Tony and Vieira, Joao (2015). *Suffrajitsu: Mrs. Pankhurst's Amazons*. The Collected Edition. Seattle, Washington: Jet City Comics.

3 Beatrice Webb

Social investigator

David Jacobs and Rosetta Morris

Beatrice Webb, née Potter, was born on 22 January 1858, to Richard and Laurencina Potter (Muggeridge and Adams, 1968; Polkingham and Thomson, 1998). She was the eighth of nine daughters and the product of an elite society. She lived in beautiful homes with servants, from one season to the next, and enjoyed the privileges of high society. Her early childhood education was provided by governesses. Subsequently, she educated herself by reading a wide array of books on various subjects, including religion and philosophy. According to Muggeridge and Adam (1968, p. 49), she was concerned about equality at the early age of 15, when she visited Brigham Young's Mormon Tabernacle in Salt Lake City and scorned the inferior treatment of the leaders' wives. At 16, she declared that she was fascinated by Joaquin Miller's writings on the influence of civilisation on progress and nations. By the time she was 21 years old, she wrote in her diary that she was going to live a serious life to help fulfil the "law of progress". She was soon to become "improvident, unconventional, non-conformist" (Muggeridge and Adams, 1968: p. 11), determined to tear down the old order and make way for the new.

Webb was a prolific author and student of organizations, who challenged the myopia of many neoclassical economists by investigating the actual conditions of the British working class. She explored the practices and institutions of working-class neighbourhoods neglected by the middle class. She pioneered empirical approaches in the social sciences and provided a remarkable example of engaged scholarship.

As with any writer, it is profitable to situate Webb's ideas, practices and personality in a social and historical context. Her demonstrated values, roles and intellectual contributions reveal an individual engaged in a dialogue with her environment. Following Jacobs (2007), it would be appropriate to find Webb's values in transition from the elitist pole to the "humanist-participatory" egalitarian alternative as she traversed multiple roles from privileged hostess to charity worker to social scientist and social reformer.

Webb described her multiple "apprenticeships", her partnerships, studies and shared projects with such individuals as Herbert Spencer, Charles Booth and Sidney Webb. The title of Webb's autobiography, *My Apprenticeship*, is apt (Webb, 1938). Therefore, it seems fitting to seek to evaluate her evolving values, her many roles, contributions in ideas and practices, as well as the multiple contexts she explored.

Among other interests, Webb had a passion for study and investigation, possibly following the unfulfilled aspirations of her mother, who died at a relatively early age. She was increasingly willing to place herself in unfamiliar contexts, to experiment, to travel through disparate cultures and cross organizational boundaries. Her privileged upbringing and close relationship with her father provided her with a foundation for self-confidence, but also preserved a vestige of elitism that inflected her social consciousness.

We must admit that we write about Webb with tremendous sympathy and many shared values. We do not, however, intend to overlook her shortcomings and contradictions. While she demonstrated an increasing awareness of social questions over the course of her career, she could not entirely escape her background, which led to limitations in her understanding of working-class agency and appropriate social-change strategies.

Refusing domestic servitude

Webb's autobiography describes her upbringing and informal education in detail. She describes devoted and cultured parents with a shortage of curiosity about the lives of their servants or the conditions of workers more broadly. Webb writes of her kind that they were accustomed to being in command. Her parents had inherited the resources for a life of leisure only to suffer a financial misfortune. Her father grew successful as a railroad executive and provided a comfortable life for Webb and her eight sisters, as well as many opportunities for fine dining with prominent politicians and intellectuals, so she discovered the reality of working-class life largely on her own.

Webb lacked formal education but enjoyed the traditional rituals of social engagement of a woman of her class. Additionally, she travelled abroad with her father on business trips and benefitted from mentoring by writers and thinkers. There was often a dialectic at work in which she grew to challenge the expectations of her acquaintances. For example, she fell in love with a radical Member of Parliament, Joseph Chamberlain, who offered her the life of a hostess at the highest levels of British society. While she had initially expected a life of comfortable domesticity, the courtship must have clarified her desire for autonomy, for which she was prepared to sacrifice love. Her passion for investigation and later advocacy necessarily undermined a purely domestic role. Curiously she never felt rich, always financially constrained, but she was always aware of her power over others, the power to command without needing to obey.

In 1883, Webb turned to a traditional role for her class and sought to address the problems of poverty through work with the Charity Organization Society. She also temporarily replaced her sister Kate as a rent collector in the model dwellings of the East End Dwellings Company. Rather than satisfy her desire to serve, over time these experiences contributed to a disenchantment with charity as a remedy for poverty. Webb was soon to move far beyond this model of Christian ministry to a willingness to attack the structural problems that underlay poverty, as would be dictated by her investigations.

In her "A Lady's View of Unemployment at the East" published in the *Pall Mall Gazette* (Webb, 1886), Webb revealed both her consciousness of her exalted status and the trajectory of her investigations:

> I am a rent collector on a large block of working-class dwellings situated near the London Docks, designed and adapted to house the lowest class of the working poor. The rooms are chiefly let in single tenements, and the tenants are for the most part casual workers, dock labourers, carmen, employees of the building trades, fish porters and hangers-on to the numberless small industries which exist in East London ... I have been enabled to inquire into the present life and previous history of a small but representative section of the vaguely defined class who are known as the "unemployed" ... Half a century ago, sack making, gun making and other handwork industries flourished in the waterside districts of London, employed thousands, and, if we may trust the memory of inhabitants, paid them well. With the introduction of machinery, the cheapening of transit, the increase of metropolitan rates and taxes, and from other economical causes these industries have forsaken the metropolis and moved into the country and suburban districts.

Webb noticed that changing jobs did not necessarily mean a corresponding move for employees and thereby derived an insight that challenged the neoclassical view of labour markets (with expectations of mobility).

Science, society and Herbert Spencer

In her autobiography, Webb described what she learned from her dialogue with Herbert Spencer, an influential writer and family friend. She had assisted him in his survey of natural phenomena, as informed by his understanding of natural selection. Webb initially accepted Spencer's belief in the unity of natural and social phenomena, his characterisation of the "whole of the processes of nature, from the formation of a crystal to the working of the party system within a democratic state" (Webb, 1926, p. 27).

Webb was able to assess Spencer's contribution to her thinking – he encouraged her to regard social institutions as akin to plants and animals, rife for classification and explanation, in the throes of processes susceptible to identification and prediction. She retained this concern for causal relations among social phenomena even as she questioned Spencer's larger analysis. Weaknesses within Spencer's thought propelled her to a new analysis:

> This generalisation illuminated my mind; the importance of functional adaptation was, for instance, at the basis of a good deal of the faith in collective regulation that I afterwards developed. Once engaged in the application of the scientific method to the facts of social organization, in my observations of East End life, of co-operation, of Factory Acts, of Trade Unionism, I shook myself completely free from laisser-faire bias – in fact I suffered from a somewhat violent reaction from it.
>
> (Webb, 1926, p. 38)

One sees a dialectic in miniature. Webb learned to apply the scientific method in a critique of Spencer's questionable "survival of the fittest" formulation. She ultimately called Spencer's work "casuistry" in its pejorative sense, that is, misapplication of poorly specified principles.

> Partly in order to gain [Spencer's] approbation and partly out of sheer curiosity about the working of his mind, I started out to discover, and where observation failed, to invent, illustrations of such scraps of theory as I understood. What I learnt from this game was ... whether the sample facts I brought him came within the "law" he wished to illustrate.
>
> (Webb, 1926, p. 27)

Thus, the apprentice learned from the "master", but learned his limitations as well. In particular, Webb discovered "a mental deformity", a mismatch between the notable development of certain intellectual faculties and the underdevelopment of his "sympathetic and emotional qualities". (Webb, 1926, p. 30).

Spencer had asked Webb to be his literary executor, but this decision could not stand once Webb agreed to marry Fabian socialist Sidney Webb. They amicably agreed to a formal dissolution of the arrangement, preserving Spencer's reputation among his ideological allies, but Webb agreed to assist with the project without acknowledgement.

From Herbert Spencer, Webb derived the concept of social evolution, but she stripped it of its reactionary meaning. She had also studied August Comte, whose optimistic and collectivist philosophy countered Spencer's classical liberalism. Both Spencer and Comte embraced scientific progress and the promise of a new society, but disagreed fundamentally about the character of the emerging society. Spencer was dismayed by Webb's growing engagement with the working class, whom he regarded as victims of their defective nature and ignorant of the requirements of liberty.

Charles Booth and the discovery of the working class

Following her break with Joseph Chamberlain and experience with the Charity Organization Society, Webb accepted a position with Charles Booth to assist with his study and survey of London East End workers. Booth's survey actually found a larger percentage of London poor, 30 percent, than socialist H. M. Hyndman had estimated. Booth applied the London School Board notion of the poverty line, which was implicitly a challenge to the equilibrium notions of classical/neoclassical orthodoxy. He was no socialist and remained an exponent of individualism even as Webb drew different conclusions.

Among other topics, Webb explored the conditions of dock workers, tailors and Jewish immigrants, and published much of her work in *The Nineteenth Century*. Webb subjected her assumptions to challenge through direct investigation and demonstrated extraordinary self-consciousness in her diary of the period.

Webb and Booth investigated working-class life, initially because of discomfiture about their class position and a desire to combat socialists. Booth, like many of his class, had grown concerned about the welfare of the working poor, but he was loathe to abandon his individualist principles. (He came to find solace among workers as a pleasing contrast with his own middle-class community.) He must have experienced some dissonance between his increasing identification with workers and his discomfort with their collectivist ideology. Such dissonance was common among the affluent, whose distance from the grim sources of their accumulated capital gave them leave to perceive injustice.

In *My Apprenticeship*, Webb (1926, p. 42) explained that she had initially viewed labor as an abstraction, in keeping with her father's assessment of its role, or a resource like water: "each individual a repetition of the other." Her prior assumptions slowly dissolved in her early morning visits to the docks. Webb met an articulate socialist dock worker who explained the indignities of the employment system (Nord, 1985, p. 161).

Webb wrote *A Lady's View of the Unemployed* (Webb, 1886) early in her investigations. More contact with the workers themselves brought ever more sympathy. Over time, her focus on empirical investigations of working-class poverty became mixed with advocacy of social change. In her mind, collectivist solutions were brewing, although she was inclined to make distinctions between the worthy and unworthy poor, the hard-working and a semi-criminal element.

The certainties of classical liberalism depend upon a blindness to people's material circumstances. A conversation with members of a marginalised working-class family shake those certainties. Some will seize upon defects of character to reassure themselves about the proper workings of markets. However, others will begin to perceive the causes of social and economic dislocation. Webb's time in working-class London, including a spell undercover arranged with the help of relatives, placed her "within sight of destitution" (Webb, 1914b: ii).

My Apprenticeship also demonstrates Webb's acute understanding of the social organization of the affluent. Of London Society, she wrote:

> London Society appeared as a shifting mass of miscellaneous and uncertain membership; it was essentially a body that could be defined, not by its circumference, which could not be traced, but by its centre or centres; centres of social circles representing or epitomising certain dominant forces within the British governing class. There was the Court, representing national tradition and custom; there was the Cabinet and ex-Cabinet, representing political power; there was a mysterious group of millionaire financiers representing money; there was the racing set – or was it the Jockey Club? ... these matters – representing sport. All persons who habitually entertained and who were entertained by the members of any one of these key groups could claim to belong to London Society. These four inner circles crossed and recrossed each other owing to an element of common membership .... Surrounding and solidifying these four intersecting social circles was a curiously tough substance – the British aristocracy – an aristocracy, as a foreign diplomatist once remarked to me, "the most talented, the most energetic and the most vulgar in the world".
>
> (Webb, 1926, p. 46)

Here, Webb registered important insights for organization studies, as she distinguished between alternate hierarchies and power centers. She was developing a class analysis, not one driven mechanistically by class struggle as Marx would have it, and she did not propose class struggle as remedy. However, Webb necessarily engaged in an indirect dialog with Marx in diagnosis and intervention.

From investigation to institution-building

Webb found herself increasingly committed to advocacy on behalf of the exploited working class. Booth's study was not the appropriate vehicle for such activism. Webb found a partner in civil servant Sidney Webb (who would become her co-author and spouse) and a set of shared projects with the Socialist Fabian Society.

The Webbs collaborated on a series of books: *The History of Trade Unionism* (1894; rev. ed. 1920), *Industrial Democracy* (1897), *English Local Government* (9 vol., 1906–29), *Consumers' Cooperative Movement* (1921) and *Soviet Communism: A New Civilization?* (2 vol., 1935). They wrote publications for the Fabian Society, proposing socialist reforms achieved peacefully through parliamentary action. They entertained political leaders at dinner, hoping to win them to reform ("permeation"). Their *Minority Report* on the so-called "Poor Law" represented a thoroughgoing critique of social welfare policy (see below). They joined the Labour Party and agitated on its behalf. One important intellectual contribution of the Webbs was to identify the three leading means for the labour movement to advance its aims: collective bargaining (a phrase coined by Webb), mutual insurance (as in cooperative self-help) and legal enactment. (Once they formed a partnership, their individual contributions were more difficult to distinguish.)

Sidney and Beatrice contributed to the creation of a few alternative institutions: the London School of Economics, to counter the orthodox laissez-faire economics centered at Cambridge, *The New Statesman*, as an organ of socialist opinion and a Parliamentary Labour Club to provide inexpensive meeting facilities for newly elected labour MPs and their wives. Add these to the Webbs' early stress on permeation and one finds that they were preoccupied with elite opinion and elite strategies. Despite their study and defense of cooperation and collective bargaining, they may have shortchanged the role of working-class agency.

It is important to identify the Webbs' contributions to economic theory. Triangulating between Marxism and T. H. Marshall's neoclassical marginal analysis, they provided an alternative model of low-wage exploitation based on unequal bargaining power, "rents" primarily to the advantage of professional and managerial workers, a "pyramid" of differential opportunity and the externalisation of social costs on workers and communities. They proposed a potential remedy in "efficiency wages", an equilibrium of higher wages and improved performance (Webb and Webb, 1902). Their social costs critique illuminated the impact of workers' dependence upon wage employment on worker health and community welfare. (See Bruce Kaufman's [2013] account of the Webbs' contributions to institutional economics.)

The term efficiency wages refers to higher-than-market determined wages. The foundation of the idea is that wages do not depend only on deterministic equilibria in demand and supply, but also on choices and implicit or explicit bargains (Webb and Webb, 1902). The central focus of efficiency wage theory is that wages are not fully determined by market forces and that higher wages potentially improve the wellbeing of workers and increase productivity. The efficiency wages concept represents recognition of the impact of reciprocity on employee–employer relations, and contains the Webbs' developing humanistic and egalitarian perspective in miniature (the humanist-participatory paradigm [Jacobs, 2007])

The Webbs (1898) noted that workers had a disadvantageous bargaining position and therefore lacked influence on health, comfort and industrial efficiency. Beatrice Webb was particularly concerned about conditions of employment under the "sweating system": very low wages, long hours of labor and unsanitary workplaces. The Webbs (1902, pp. 710–711) proposed that a higher standard of life would enable higher levels of performance and enhance organizational effectiveness as compared with the depressed vitality and productivity of exploited workers. Webb and Webb (1902) posited a theory of exchange in which the quality of work and the generosity of compensation are understood as interdependent. They struggled against dominant economic philosophies that pronounced the inevitability of working-class poverty, whether determined by an "iron law of subsistence", a fixed "wage fund", supply and demand or marginal product (Ross, 1991, p. 173).

Webb and Webb (1902) believed that increased wages at the expense of profits would improve rather than reduce productivity. Their investigation of several industries involving 110,000 employees showed that higher wages did not interfere with the profitability of the industries (Webb, 1912). Instead, over a 16-year period of efficiency wages, the number of factories grew by 60 percent and the number of employees doubled. The results of this investigation support the proposition that efficiency wages improve productivity.

Several other investigators have found similar results in more recent studies (Feldstein, 2008; Holzer, 1990; Levine, 1992; Mas, 2006; Reich et al., 2003; Riley and Bondibene, 2017). Additionally, research shows that higher wages increase the quality of production (Cowherd and Levine, 1992) and customer service (Fisher et al., 2006), and as real wages fall, productivity becomes stagnant (Blundell, Crawford and Jin, 2014).

The Webbs' research partnership is illustrated in this passage:

> To spend hour after hour in the chancel of an old parish church, in the veiled light of an ancient monument, in the hard little office of a

solicitor, in the ugly and bare anteroom of the council chamber of a local authority, or even in a dungeon without ventilation or daylight ... with a stack of manuscripts, or a pile of printed volumes, to get through in a given time, induces an indescribably stimulated state of mind.

(Webb and Webb, 2010)

Their co-authored book, *Methods of Social Study*, was highly commended by economist Alfred Marshall, among others. Bruce Kaufman (2013) describes the Webbs' work as "exhaustive on-the-ground investigation, an inductive/empiricist approach to theory development, a corpus of theory integrating in a literary way ideas and insights from diverse writers and disciplines (Smith, Marx, Marshall; economics, sociology, history), and a progressive policy program emphasizing social control and reengineering of institutions to produce more efficient and equitable outcomes".

On the Poor Law

As a member of the Royal Commission on the Poor Law from 1905 to 1910 (Webb, 1948, p. 18), Webb proposed programs for a minimum standard of life: a national old age pension, medical relief via public health authorities, and a program to deal with unemployment (Muggeridge and Adams, 1968). While her proposals (rejected by the Commission) anticipated the Beveridge Commission recommendations and would have radically enhanced the generosity of the British State, Webb's possibly more authoritarian side was evident in this provision:

If it was discovered by actual observation of the man's present behavior that there was in him a grave moral defect not otherwise remediable, he would have to submit himself, in a detention colony, to a treatment which would be at once curative and deterrent ...

(Muggeridge and Adams, 1968, p. 177)

On the other hand, this unfortunate reference to detention colonies, a discordant note in an otherwise compassionate document, may have been a concession to political realities (Webb and Webb, 1973; Leopold, 2017).

A growing feminist critique

Many have denied that Beatrice Webb was a feminist, noting comments affirming female domesticity and discounting women's suffrage in her youth. Seymour-Jones (1992, p. 206) argues that Webb accepted Herbert Spencer's belief in women's evolutionary and moral inferiority. On the other hand, Nyland (1994) examines Webb's works for *New Statesman* from 1913 to 1929 and finds contrary evidence. He submits that she came to endorse a partnership among human beings in human affairs. According to Nyland, Webb understood the parallels between the women's struggle, the labour struggle and the resistance of subject races victimised by imperialism. Her claim for equal wages for women was informed by a working-class understanding of employers' willingness to set women against men in pursuit of profits. She comprehended the deficiencies of a bourgeois feminism focused on the rights of middle-class women and appreciated other fault lines of exploitation. Webb appeared to develop a consciousness of marginalised, oppressed peoples despite the mainstream views of markets and Empire. (However, there is no doubt that the Webbs and other Fabians retained a degree of commitment to the British imperial project.)

Deborah Nord's book characterises Webb's contradictions in this way:

> Webb was a "religious" Fabian, an "emancipated" woman who rejected political feminism, an apparent anti-Semite who strongly identified with Jews, a non-Marxist admirer of Soviet Russia, a class snob who married 'beneath' her and felt most at home among Lancashire textile workers, an ambitious woman who gave up personal, individual notoriety for fame in partnership.
>
> (Nord, 1985, pp. 12–13)

One of the reasons writers advance rather different accounts of Webb's views is that they were not fixed. *My Apprenticeship* (Webb, 1926) reveals an active mind registering contradictions and seeking resolution through new approaches.

Deficits in social consciousness?

Webb's initial strategy for socialist reform depended upon influencing the programs of political elites through dinner and discussion. Later, the Webbs turned to the Labour Party. Gertrude Himmelfarb, a 20th-century historian, delighted in mocking Beatrice Webb's Fabian elitism:

> one hears the voice of Mrs. Webb threatening to legislate out of the Socialist Commonwealth the parasites of society. When guests rise hungrily from her meager dinner-table to engage in the purposeful conversation in which she firmly directs them, one realizes how entirely in keeping this is with the austere regimen of life and labor she would have imposed on the citizens of her good society. And the unobtrusive attendance at these dinner parties of the proper complement of properly

attired servants recalls her conception of the ideal social order, in which an equality, preferably a minimal equality, of goods would cohere with a substantial inequality of persons.

(Himmelfarb, 1968)

In part, this is a standard critique of social regulation. The advocate of "free markets" finds liberty always at risk under government, but never challenged by private authority. Some have, however, questioned Webb's apparent emphasis on elite agency. While Webb investigated the cooperative spirit and union solidarity in working-class neighborhoods, she was skeptical about the sufficiency of the initiatives of workers themselves. What perhaps was lacking was further dialogue with the dockworkers, or with William Morris or H. M. Hyndman as exponents of working-class institutions. By no means are we faulting her for failing to idealise an imaginary working class. However, eccentric middle-class reformers could not be a substitute for an engaged public; extended democracy is not an elite project.

American labour scholar Selig Perlman (1970, pp. 9–10) noted the multiple ways in which intellectuals have treated the working class "as an undifferentiated mass in the grip of an abstract force".

The other types of intellectuals in and close to the labor movement, the 'ethical' type, the heirs of Owen and the Christian Socialists, and the 'social efficiency' type, best represented by the Fabians ... have equally with the orthodox Marxists reduced labour to a mere abstraction.

Perlman, of course, may have been guilty of the same sort of reification of a particular notion of labour movement in his claims about "job consciousness".

William Morris criticised the Fabian strategy of permeation as unsuited to radical change, and defended a socialism rooted in working-class craft communities. One might have wished for more dialogue between the Webbs and Morris in the pursuit of democratic models of social change.

In the last decade of her life, Webb was depressed and disillusioned by the First World War and by the shortcomings of Labour, the party in power. She was pessimistic about the future of British society. Perhaps she felt a need for a new inspiration, not entirely rational, but religious in its reassurance. She and Sidney, charitably and incongruously, embraced the economic achievements of the Soviet State. They were not advocates of revolution by any means. They appear to have evaluated the Soviet experiment from the top down, without attention to dissident voices. The Webbs' relatively uncritical stance may have reflected their elitism. They failed to employ social investigation with regard to Soviet institutions and allowed theory to desensitise them to the exploitation of workers under the system. Economic theory might have blinded even the Webbs to circumstances inside organizations.

On the other hand, Webb described some misgivings about the Soviet State in her diary. She worried about repression and authoritarianism and wondered, "how can we reconcile this dominance of a religious order imposing on all citizens a new orthodoxy, with the freedom of the soul of man?" (Nord 1985, p. 245). The source of the dilemma was "orthodoxy", which had been the target of her critical analysis before in the case of laissez-faire.

With regard to Webb's contributions, sociologist Mary Ann Romano (1998) explains that she applied the components of the scientific method: experiment, hypothesis and verification, to the study of social problems. With the assistance of her husband, Sidney, she sought to bring the scientific method to government. At the same time, she employed socialist doctrine in the attempt to solve social problems. One can see that the Webbs' attraction to the Soviet State represented a collision between science and doctrine.

Falling out of bed

Webb's lifetime of growth and revelation reminds us of a passage in Lincoln Steffens' autobiography (Steffens, 2005), in which he spoke of "falling out of bed", by which he meant an epiphany with which he re-evaluated his ideology and alliances. Steffens ended his life with a curious openness to the politics of Roosevelt and Stalin at the same time. Webb seems to have had a series of these epiphanies, including her studies, – and increasing disagreement – with Herbert Spencer, her abortive courtship with MP Joseph Chamberlain, her varying approaches to the working poor, her convergence to socialism (and partnership with Sidney Webb) and her ambiguous attraction to the Soviet model.

Patricia Meyer Spacks (as cited in [Nord, 1985, p. 13]) says of Webb that she was a woman suspended between feeling and reason, love and work, "feminine" emotion and "masculine" intellect. The specifics aside, it is certainly accurate to describe Webb as a thinker with ideas in flux, powered by contradictions of theory and practice and informed by a multiplicity of roles and contexts (Spacks, 1976).

Despite the shortcomings of her socialist praxis, Webb provides an excellent model of the organizational theorist. She described and theorised about a variety of working-class institutions, neglected by other organizational scholars of the time. (Such institutions were invisible to many middle-class thinkers, except insofar as they were an affront to free market ideals.) In partnership with Sidney, she identified various forms of labour organization and their disparate strategies. The Webbs studied the history of trade unionism, blending historical inquiry with empirical social science. As they explained, research should begin with "an exhaustive examination of the structure and function of the social institution itself" and incorporate a consideration of the "effects of all factors whatsoever, mental physical and social, to whatever sister science these factors may predominantly belong" (Webb and Webb, 1948, p. 155).

Webb helped establish participant observation as a legitimate and effective method of organizational study. In fact, she troubled to immerse herself in environments scorned by her academic colleagues. Her historical inquiry and social investigation led her to social insight and advocacy.

Contrary to the then-popular belief that poverty was a result of a moral failure and indiscriminate charity, Webb countered that the causes of poverty were institutional (Muggeridge and Adams, 1968, p. 181). In her contextual analysis, she anticipated elements of systems theory. The Webbs' theory of efficiency wages illuminated the possible interactions of organizations, individuals and society.

It may be that Webb's increasing attention to social engineering limited the appreciation of her contributions to sociology and organizational studies. T.S. Simey (1961) writes of a transition in the Webbs' writing, in which deduction and advocacy qualified their emphasis on inductive reasoning. It is not surprising, however, that social investigation in 19th-century England would lead to something other than dispassionate study.

Having ventured into hidden realms of exploitation, Webb had the audacity to combine illuminating scholarship with calls for radical social change. One wonders what her contributions would have been given another decade or a more recent moment.

Further reading

Original text by Beatrice Webb

Webb, B. (1926). *My Apprenticeship*. London: Longmans, Green & Co.

Key academic text

Nyland, C. (1994). *Beatrice Webb as a Feminist*. Department of Economics, University of Wollongong, Working Paper 94–3, 1994, 31. http://ro.uow.edu.au/commwkpapers/280. Accessed on 27 February 2018.

Accessible resource

LSE Digital Library. (2018). *The Webbs on the Web*. https://digital.library.lse.ac.uk/collections/webb. Accessed on 30 April 2019.

References

Blundell, R., Crawford, C. and Jin, W. (2014). What can wages and employment tell us about the UK productivity puzzle? *The Economic Journal*, 124(576), 377–407.

Cowherd, D.M. and Levine, D.I. (1992). Product quality and pay equity between lower-level employees and top management: An investigation of distributive justice theory. *Administrative Science Quarterly*, 37(2), 302–320.

Feldstein, M. (2008). Did wages reflect growth in productivity? *Journal of Policy Modeling*, 30(4), 591–594.

Fisher, M., Krishnan, J. and Netessine, S. (2006). *Retail Store Execution: An Empirical Study*. Operations and Information Management Department, The Wharton School, University of Pennsylvania.

Himmelfarb, G. (1968). Beatrice Webb, A life. *Commentary*. https://www.commenta rymagazine.com/articles/beatrice-webb-a-life-1858-1943-by-kitty-muggeridge-and-ruth-adam/. Accessed on 27 February 2018.

Holzer, H.J. (1990). Wages, employer costs, and employee performance in the firm. *Industrial and Labor Relations Review*, 43(3), 147–164.

Jacobs, D. (2007). Critical biography and management education. *Academy of Management Learning and Education*, 6(1), 104–108.

Kaufman, B.E. (2013). Sidney and Beatrice Webb's institutional theory of labor markets and wage determination. *Industrial Relations*, 52, 765–791.

Leopold, P.M. (2017). Problem of destitution in the United Kingdom. http://lawi.org .uk/problem-of-destitution/.

Levine, D.I. (1992). Can wage increases pay for themselves? Test with a production function. *Economic Journal*, 102(414), 1102–1115.

Mas, A. (2006). Pay, reference points, and police performance. *Quarterly Journal of Economics*, 121(3), 783–821.

Muggeridge, K. and Adam, R. (1968). *Beatrice Webb: A life, 1858–1943*. Chicago: Academy Chicago.

Nord, D.E. (1985). *The Apprenticeship of Beatrice Webb*. Amherst, MA: The University of Massachusetts Press.

Nyland, C. (1994). *Beatrice Webb as a Feminist*. Department of Economics, University of Wollongong, Working Paper 94–3, 1994, 31. http://ro.uow.edu.au/ commwkpapers/280. Accessed on 27 February 2018.

Perlman, S. (1970). *A Theory of the Labor Movement*. New York: Augustus M. Kelley.

Polkingham, B. and Thomson, D.L. (1998). Beatrice Webb: 1858–1943. In Polkingham, B. and Narayan, U., *Adam Smith's Daughters*. Northampton, MA: Edward Elgar Publishing, Inc, pp. 51–68.

Reich, M., Hall, P. and Jacobs, K. (2003). *Living Wages and Economic Performance: The San Francisco Airport Model*. Berkeley: Institute of Industrial Relations, University of California.

Riley, R. and Bondibene, C. (2017). Raising the standard: Minimum wage and firm productivity. *Labour Economics*, 44(C), 27–50.

Romano, M.A. (1998). *Beatrice Webb, 1858–1943: The Socialist with a Sociological Imagination*. Lewiston, NY: E. Mellen.

Ross, D. (1991), *The Origins of American Social Science*. Cambridge: Cambridge University Press.

Seymour-Jones, C. (1992). *Beatrice Webb: Woman of Conflict*. London: Allison and Busby.

Simey, T.S. (1961). The contributions of Sidney and Beatrice Webb to sociology. *British Journal of Sociology*, 12(2), 106–123.

Spacks, P.A.M. (1976). *The Female Imagination*. New York: Avon Books.

Steffens, L. (2005). *The Autobiography of Lincoln Steffens*. Berkeley, CA: Heyday Books.

Webb, B. (1886). A lady's view of the unemployed at the East. *Pall Mall Gazette*, (6530), http://webbs.library.lse.ac.uk/934/.

Webb, B. (1926). *My Apprenticeship*. London: Longmans, Green & Co.

Webb, B. (1948). *Our Partnership*. Barbara Drake and Margaret I. Cole (eds.). London: Longman Green & Co.

Webb, S. (1912). The economic theory of a legal minimum wage. *The Journal of Political Economy*, 20(10), 973–998.

Webb, S. and Webb, B. (1898). *Problems of Modern Industry*. New York: Longmans, Green & Co.

Webb, S. and Webb, B. (1902). *Industrial Democracy*. London: Longman Green & Co.

Webb, S. and Webb, B. (1973). *English Poor Law Policy*. Clifton, NJ: A.M. Kelley.

Webb, S. and Webb, B. (2010). *Methods of Social Study*. Cambridge: Cambridge University Press.

4 "There is always something that one can do"

Social engineering and organization in the family politics of Alva Myrdal

Louise Wallenberg and Torkild Thanem

In this chapter, we introduce the work and writings of 20th-century Swedish politician, diplomat and public intellectual Alva Myrdal (1902–1986). Although Myrdal's work has been completely neglected in organization studies, its organizational implications are significant. Myrdal's social democrat family politics was based on a bizarre combination of feminist and eugenic social engineering, which shaped the organization of the Swedish welfare state and advanced women's participation in the labour market. Myrdal also became a role model of women's leadership in public life: she was vice president of the International Federation of Business and Professional Women between 1938 and 1947; she headed the United Nations' section on welfare policy between 1949 and 1950 and served as the first director of UNESCO's Social and Human Sciences Sector between 1950 and 1955; between 1956 and 1961 Myrdal was Sweden's ambassador to India and she was elected as a member of the Swedish parliament in 1962; she served as a consultative cabinet minister for disarmament in 1966 and was appointed secretary of education in 1969. In 1982, she was awarded the Nobel Peace Prize for her work in favour of disarmament (which she shared with the Mexican diplomat and politician Alfonso García Robles). In what follows, we will try and tease out the organizational dimensions of Myrdal's work by focusing on the feminist and eugenic aspects of her social engineering.

At the core of Alva Myrdal's family politics was a relentless strive to create a classless society where women and men were treated as equals, with equal opportunities to participate in paid work, politics and public life. According to Myrdal, a person's abilities were a question of nurture more than nature; rather than being given at birth, they were shaped and nurtured by social and economic conditions. In the classless society that she was hoping to create with the new welfare state, members of the working class would be just as likely to prosper as members of the upper class.

For Myrdal, eugenic birth control played a key role in this grand political project. If the new welfare state was to liberate women from the unsalaried home sphere, it needed to make sure that it had the best minds and bodies at its disposal; the best economists, engineers and social scientists, the best architects, designers and politicians. And, it needed to prevent being dragged down by social problems caused by "human matter" of inferior quality.

Eugenics enjoyed a prominent position in Swedish science and politics in the 1920s and 30s. The Swedish Society for Racial Hygiene had been founded in 1909 with the aim to shape public opinion, influence policy-making and support research. In 1922, the State Institute for Racial Biology was established, the first of its kind worldwide to be government-funded. Although the Institute failed to generate any scientific contributions concerning "racial" differences in the Swedish population, it published a number of pamphlets and coffee-table books filled with photographs displaying idealised examples of "Nordic type"–looking scientists, industrialists and peasants (Björkman and Widmalm, 2010). By the 1930s, the Institute came to replace its emphasis on racial biology with medical genetics and social medicine, but maintained a firm belief in selective reproduction and coercive sterilisation schemes. Between the 1930s and the early '60s there was a broad consensus within the Swedish population and across the Swedish political spectrum that eugenics would help produce a healthier and more able population (see e.g. Runcis, 1998).

Although Myrdal makes few explicit references to eugenics, she readily assumed that eugenic solutions would lead to a more physically and mentally fit population whilst preventing the spread of poor health and poverty. There was little room for human slack and imperfection in her view of the efficient welfare state. Everybody had to be able to do their bit in the common struggle against mental feebleness, alcoholism and other socio-medical problems.

Population crisis

In 1934, Alva Myrdal published her most famous work, *Kris i befolknings-frågan* [*Crisis in the Population Question*], which she co-authored with her husband, economist and later Nobel laureate Gunnar Myrdal. The Myrdals were alarmed that Sweden's population had failed to grow since 1920. According to their analysis, couples refrained from having children because they could not afford it and because women did not want to give up their work and professional careers (see also Etzemüller, 2012, p. 105). In this book, the Myrdals' concern with Sweden's declining birth rate led them to develop a utilitarian argument for a family politics based partly on active social policy interventions, partly on eugenic reproduction principles. The Myrdals rejected Malthusianism and Neo-Malthusianism. The poverty they were witnessing in Sweden during the early Depression years was not the result of overpopulation, but its opposite, and it had to be tackled accordingly. Starvation, delayed marriage and other "natural" birth controls would only exacerbate the problem. So would a one-sided dependence on "artificial" birth control measures such as the grand contraception schemes that Swedish Neo-Malthusians sought to impose on the working class.

In 1929, the Myrdals had been invited to the USA as Rockefeller Fellows. Visiting the universities of Columbia, Chicago and Wisconsin *inter alia*, Alva Myrdal took the opportunity to continue her studies in sociology, psychology and children's education (she had graduated from Stockholm College five years prior with a bachelor's degree in psychology). They were both startled by the social and economic conditions of the American working class, and worried that the extreme disparities and poverty levels they witnessed during their year in the USA would become reality in their home country. Alva Myrdal later noted that it was their USA experience which made them "politically conscious" (Lindskog, 1986, p. 18; our translation), and convinced them that strong government was required to solve the social, economic and demographic problems facing modern society.

The Myrdals did not endorse unlimited procreation to maximise population growth; children in large families were at a high risk of being raised under conditions of negligence and poverty, cramped together in overcrowded and unhygienic digs. Instead, the problem of Sweden's population deficit required a family politics based on a sophisticated combination of selective reproduction and social policy. The Myrdals were highly critical of Swedish legislation at the time, which prohibited public information about contraceptives (*Preventivmedelslagen* was implemented in 1911 and upheaved in 1938). Like the burgeoning Swedish sex education movement, they argued that people should only have children if they *chose* to have children. To help people make that choice the family had to become a target of government policy-making; through widespread sex education, public provision of contraception, voluntary abortion and sterilisation schemes and, in certain cases, through the employment of coercive sterilisation.

Myrdal and her husband were confident that most couples, under favourable circumstances, were capable of making the right choice for themselves. They also rejected the eugenic argument that poor families tended to have many children because the parents were lacking in "racial hygiene" and genetic constitution (see e.g. Myrdal and Myrdal, 1935 [1934], p. 231). However, in Chapter 7 of *Kris i befolkningsfrågan*, when discussing what "human quality" is required to meet the increased quality requirements of labour and production in modern society, they accept "eugenic" as well as "socio-pedagogical" grounds for sterilisation. On the whole, they are more strongly convinced by the socio-pedagogical argument for sterilisation, believing that coercive sterilisation will prevent children from being raised under unfit family conditions (ibid, p. 260). And even though their privileging of environmental explanations makes them argue that sterilisation is unlikely to eradicate the reproduction of physical and mental "defects", they are optimistic that future research in eugenics may generate additional causes for sterilisation (see Myrdal and Myrdal, 1935, pp. 258–259).

Their view on sterilisation was in line with the Swedish Sterilisation Act, which was being implemented the same year as their book was published:

> If there is reason to assume that someone suffering from insanity, imbecility or another mental impairment for that reason is deemed incapable of taking care of their future children, or will through hereditation transmit insanity or imbecility upon them, according to this Act and without his consent sterilization may be undertaken on him, because the disruption of his soul means that he permanently lacks the capacity to give valid consent to the measure.
>
> (The Sterilisation Act of 1934, quoted in Myrdal and Myrdal, 1935, p. 259; our translation)

According to the Myrdals, the enhancement of "human matter" (1935, p. 257) could be more effectively achieved through negative than positive eugenics; it would be less difficult to prevent reproduction amongst "the genetically and socially inferior" than to increase reproduction amongst "the genetically superior". It was in society's interest, they claimed, to prevent reproduction amongst "the bottom layer of mentally inferior individuals" (p. 264). As a case in point, they invoke the problem of imbecile mothers:

> Time and again we meet ... large broods of children born by unmarried imbecile mothers, where the entire hoard must be accommodated by the public, and where their frequent asociality and criminality will cause further concern in the future. That a number of such individuals are prevented from coming into the world will be a significant social relief, regardless of what effect such a restraint might have on the quality of the population.
>
> (Myrdal and Myrdal, 1935, p. 263; our translation)

At the same time, the Myrdals admitted that "defect" individuals made up a small proportion of the Swedish population. Hence, coercive sterilisation played a striking but minor role in their overall solution to the population crisis. They identified a bigger challenge in the larger group of people they regarded as "inferior" or "subprime" individuals, who were incapable of meeting the increasing quality requirements of the modern economy; since it would be too expensive to keep "subprime" individuals on social support, yet unnecessary to isolate them from society at large, the Myrdals suggested that new methods were required to ensure their integration in simple but productive work.

To increase sound reproduction in the majority of the population, however, eugenic measures were of little help. Social policy measures were required. Indeed, the Myrdals noted that social policy is the "organizational" component of a larger "sociological process of adaptation" (Myrdal and Myrdal, 1935, p. 257). The new welfare state had to make it affordable for families to have children (indeed, to have *more* children), and to raise them under stable social and economic conditions. A healthy population growth would only be possible if the government took social and economic responsibility for the wellbeing of families with small children. As Myrdal reminisces in a 1979 interview with Swedish Radio, the average Swede found it difficult to grasp this argument:

> Very few people understood that our message was twofold. On the one hand, we really stood for voluntary parenthood, for birth control, for the individual right to choose when to have children. The children who were conceived should be desired and not the result of a mistake. [...] The other message that we brought forward was that families with children, despite the increasing welfare in our country, were hit by high extra costs. Hence, they came to live under worse financial conditions than other people. We therefore argued that families must be able to decide for themselves how many children they could afford. And, if children are to be given a rational upbringing, then society must cover certain extra costs for the children.
>
> (Myrdal quoted in Lindskog, 1986, p. 42;
> our translation)

To facilitate sound reproduction and the rational collective upbringing of children, the Myrdals put forward a number of proposals, including publicly funded day care, child support and communal housing: publicly funded day care would enable mothers to continue working whilst their children were cared for by professionals; child support would reduce the economic burden on couples having children; communal housing would enable families to help each other with cooking, cleaning and other housekeeping chores. Publicly funded day care was also seen as an effective buffer against the unhealthy development of "neurotic" individualism in children; by attending public crèches, children would have to learn to interact with peers. These were largely Myrdal's ideas – Gunnar's contribution to the book consisted primarily in the economic and demographic analysis. Although only a few examples of communal housing came to see the light of day, the Swedish Social Democrat government introduced public day care in 1943; income-based child support was introduced in 1937 and general child support was implemented in 1948.

At the end of the book, the Myrdals launch the notion of "the new family", an idea most likely conceived and penned by Alva. Critical about the isolated and patriarchal family units of contemporary western cities producing a society of selfish and atomised individuals, they put forward an argument for "family organizational reform" (p. 386ff). In this new "family organization", they imagine a family household fully integrated into the "public household" of the welfare state, where women and men are equals in private and public life:

> Within this new family … the wife shall be at her husband's side as a comrade even in productive labour, and the children's right to a future life of purposefully reared existence shall again be safeguarded. During the work day … the family shall, according to the division of labour of industrial society, be separated: the adults … must be at their place of work; the children [shall] play, eat, sleep and attend school … The common home, the common leisure time and the … subtle personal relationship – which we believe constitutes the family, will remain. Private housekeeping, individualist paternalism, [and] the wife's restrained life course shall not. That must be eradicated if, and to the extent that, the family's adaptation to life requires.
>
> (Myrdal and Myrdal, 1935, pp. 389–390; our translation)

Some of the later commentators on *Kris i befolkningsfrågan* have paid more attention to the Myrdals' eugenic arguments than to the allegedly humane and feminist intentions of their family politics (see e.g. Runcis, 1998; Habel, 2002; Etzemüller, 2012, 2014). However, the Myrdals were by no means driving Swedish eugenics. The Swedish welfare state performed approximately 63,000 sterilisations between 1935 and 1975 (SOU, 1999, 2000; see also Broberg and Roll Hansen, 1996; Spektorowski and Mizrachi, 2004). Even though Sweden performed far more sterilisations on physically healthy individuals than did the other Nordic countries (Broberg and Roll Hansen, 1996; Spektorowski and Mizrachi, 2004), sterilisation was a widespread practice in a number of western countries during this period. And even though a significant number of "promiscuous women", "imbeciles" and "addicts" were sterilised on eugenic grounds, without full consent and after being subjected to pressure, persuasion or outright coercion, the majority of sterilisations in Sweden were performed voluntarily, especially towards the end of the period (ibid; see also SOU, 2000).

Woman's role in society

Alva Myrdal's feminist family politics was more strongly expressed in her sole-authored writings and in the work that she did without her husband. Already in the early 1930s, she published critical articles in journals and magazines discussing what she referred to as the "woman dilemma" (see Myrdal, 1932, 1933, 1934). The target of her critique was the patriarchal construction of what she regarded as a "fake femininity", which oppressed and subordinated women by reducing them to mothers and wives. More than twenty years later, Simone de Beauvoir articulated very similar ideas in *The Second Sex* (2011 [1949]). In Myrdal's (1934) view, the prevalence of "fake femininity" was a social problem that excluded women from the public and professional spheres. Her solution was an economic system that would make it possible for women to have children yet be able to continue working and contributing to society. These issues were further expressed in Myrdal's second book *Stadsbarn [City Children]*, which was published in 1935.

Critiquing extant child care for being limited and inadequate (the well-off were able to send their children to luxury crèches preparing them for private schooling, whilst child care for the poor was substandard), the book proposed a reform that would make child care a public good available to every family with small children. Government-funded, it would also be based on contemporary research in child psychology. Torn between advocates of "free" contra "authoritarian" child-rearing, Myrdal took a middle position. Though she was in agreement with the critics of "authoritarian" child-rearing, she maintained that "free" child-rearing provided no real alternative. Her own solution to this heated debate was a compromise where she emphasised the importance of "collaboration" between "child-rearer" and child – a caring and fostering model which would be "free" yet "authoritarian".

The following year, Myrdal was given an opportunity to put into practice what she had preached in her book: she was asked to set up and head the Socio-Pedagogical Seminar in Stockholm. She held the post until 1948, only interrupted by stints abroad and work for various government committees and commissions. With the purpose of training future preschool teachers, the Seminar was an important precursor to the preschool teacher programmes that came to be established at Swedish colleges in 1976. The student body was all female. In addition to emphasising training in child psychology and social science, Myrdal was concerned with the personal development of her students.

In 1930s Sweden, the prevailing discourse on women was deeply essentialist. Politicians and commentators across the political spectrum deemed women's fertility central in resolving the population crisis. They also tended to highlight women's natural capacity for mothering. Alva Myrdal was highly critical of these sentiments; population growth should not be dependable on women being turned into reproduction machines. According to Myrdal, it was exactly these kinds of old-fashioned misconceptions which tied women to the home sphere, prevented them from participating in paid work and public life and maintained women's subordination to men (Myrdal, 1934, 1942). In contrast, she argued that women's and men's "mental" capacities are more alike than different, and that there is no reason why women should be prevented from contributing with their full capacities outside of the home.

At the same time as Myrdal was striving to change these conditions, some of her own writing on womanhood and women's role in society undermined this position. In the text "Uppfostrad till äkta 'quinnlighet'" (1934), she is critical of women who marry to become housewives or who escape their duty to society through a one-sided pursuit of their own personal development and happiness. While she acknowledges that this is a systemic problem produced by an outmoded gendered division of labour, she seems to blame women for willingly participating in a patriarchal system. In *Nation and Family*, Myrdal ends up celebrating male thinking, agency and industriousness in ways that construe woman as the less sensible of the two sexes.

On the whole, however, Alva Myrdal may be seen as the key architect of a modern and egalitarian "gender system" that has increasingly, albeit imperfectly, shaped the lives and careers of Swedish women and men. Maintaining that women and men were "different but equal", Myrdal envisioned a modernised society where women were able to partake in public life with the same rights and opportunities as men, and devote themselves to paid professional work on *a par* with men, even if they chose to marry and have children. For a number of decades, women's participation in Swedish society has been facilitated by a public child-care reform which she devised. But for this to work properly, Myrdal pursued two more ideas, which remain to become dominant practice: the "new family man" and the six-hour work day.

Myrdal's notion of the new family man was that of a man who regarded his private role in the home sphere as being of equal importance to his public role in the sphere of professional work, politics and community engagement. He was a father who would share the house chores with his wife and be present with his children. According to Myrdal, the six-hour work day was a prerequisite to make this possible. Myrdal argued that the shorter work day, government-funded to avoid negative consequences on the family economy, had a number of benefits. She explains this in an interview from 1979:

> It does not only mean that those who now work eight hours go down to six. It also means that those who are unemployed can start to work. [...] It would even lead to more ... togetherness for men and women [...] both parties would come home without being totally worn out. Instead they could direct their attention and feelings towards each other, their home, their children, their local community and their neighbours. It would give so much more togetherness in one's life. And I dare say that it would yield a much higher quality of life, and more happiness
>
> (quoted in Lindskog, 1986, p. 48; our translation)

Alva Myrdal's altruistic utilitarianism

Alva Myrdal's politics were unlikely to have been unaffected by her own experiences. As a young woman, she struggled to participate in paid professional work on equal terms with her male peers. One year after the publication of *Kris i befolkningsfrågan*, the Swedish government set up a population commission. Gunnar was given a prominent position. Myrdal was asked to come in a couple of times to act as an external reviewer and comment on the sociological effects of family size. This irritated her, and she would later express how disappointed she felt when realising that she was not given the same opportunities as Gunnar just because she was a woman; even though she worked so hard, she "still was not offered a job" (Hirdman, 2002, p. 12; our translation).

However, her personal experience cannot fully explain Myrdal's engagement in family politics, social engineering and the organization of the Swedish welfare state. Throughout her life, Myrdal was driven by a sense of empathy, devotion and responsibility. She felt strongly for the disadvantaged, especially the women and children she observed living in poor unsanitary conditions, without access to proper care and education. Yet, she felt she would be able to do more if channelling her empathy and expertise towards a grander rational purpose. On 3 January 1940, she notes in her diary that "I find myself brooding night and day – especially at night – over what I will do with my life so as to accomplish something really useful. I have spent so much time thinking about it that it is sure to lead to something" (quoted in Hirdman, 2008, p. vii). Indeed, Myrdal's resume testifies that she was remarkably capable of making herself useful; to improve the situation for women, to stop the arms race, to protect democracy, to help children in need.

Perhaps Myrdal's project is best summarised by the term "altruistic utilitarianism": she was driven by a combined desire to help others and to be useful. But like all benevolent projects, Myrdal's was not unequivocally good. Her good intentions did not produce unequivocally good consequences for all. In 1999, the Swedish parliament decided to offer economic compensation to the victims of Sweden's coercive sterilisation scheme. By 2002, the Swedish government had made pay-outs to 1,595 people (*Sydsvenskan*, 2003). Though one should be careful not to blame Myrdal and her husband for Sweden's comprehensive sterilisation policy, she verbally supported the sterilisation of "imbeciles" and "the insane", some of whom were granted economic retribution decades later. Certain of her own capacity to do the right thing, that is, the most "sensible" thing, she argued that it is "Our duty as responsible politicians ... to use the power that has been handed to us, and to use it maximally and as rationally as possible" (in Lindskog, 1986, p. 22; our translation).

In late December 1979, shortly before her illness left her silent and unable to express her social and political engagement, she came back to her life-long conviction, that as individuals we can always do *something* to improve our conditions, as long as we apply our reason:

> There are only two things that I know for sure. First, there is nothing to be won from trying to avoid difficulties and to give into wishful thinking. And second, there is always something that one can do. My humble urging would then entail: to study, to try and explore various solutions and to compare the results – even if they are only part solutions. If we do not do this, we might as well just surrender. And it is not decent to surrender
>
> (quoted in Lindskog, 1986, p. 3;
> our translation; our emphasis)

Looking back, it is easy to view Myrdal as a paradoxical character. Her struggle to engineer and organize a more egalitarian society was a profoundly elitist project that ended up oppressing and excluding the people who already suffered the most from the inequalities and injustices that she sought to bring to an end. In this respect, she was very much a product of her time, and her elitist manner and politics strike a discord with the grassroots activism that has characterised later generations of feminism.

However, Myrdal's impact has endured. Through her prolific writing, her pioneering work in education and child care and her many leadership positions in international organizations and Swedish government, she conceived a number of ideas and policy measures that challenged patriarchal structures, reorganized social and economic relations between women and men and continue to facilitate women's participation in work, politics and public life. Myrdal was a tempered radical who achieved radical change through mainstream institutions. She may have dressed and looked like a femocrat, but her unselfish devotion to social progress is in stark contrast to contemporary femocrats who seem to care about little but their own careers. While we are not convinced that such elitism would prove effective today, the kind of anti-essentialism that Myrdal pursued remains crucial in challenging entrenched structures of inequality, oppression and injustice, within and beyond the realm of formal work organizations.

Further readings

Original texts by Alva Myrdal

Myrdal, Alva (1941) *Nation and Family: The Swedish Experiment in Democratic Family and Population Policy*. New York: Harper.
Myrdal, Alva (1942) Kvinnovärde och kvinnokult. *Idun*, no. 23.
Myrdal, Alva and Klein, Viola (1956) *Women's Two Roles: Home and Work*. London: Routledge. (Reprinted 2001.)

Key academic text

Ekerwald, Hedvig (2000) Alva Myrdal: Making the private public. *Acta Sociologica* 43(4): 343–352.

Accessible Resource

Hirdman, Yvonne (2008) *Alva Myrdal: The Passionate Mind*. Bloomington: Indiana University Press.

References

Beauvoir, Simone de (2011 [1949]) *The Second Sex*, translated by Constance Borde and Sheila Malovany-Chevallier. New York: Vintage.
Björkman, Maria and Widmalm, Sven (2010) Selling eugenics: The case of Sweden. *Notes & Records of the Royal Society* 64: 379–400.
Broberg, G. and Roll-Hansen, N. (1996) *Eugenics and the Welfare State*. Ann Arbor, MI: University of Michigan Press.
Etzemüller, Thomas (2012) Rationalizing the individual – engineering society: The case of Sweden. In Kerstin Brückweh, Benjamin Ziemann, Dirk Schumann and Richard F. Wetzell (eds.) *Engineering Society: The Role of the Human and Social Sciences in Modern Societies, 1880–1980*, pp. 97–118. Basingstoke: Palgrave.
Etzemüller, Thomas (2014) *Alva and Gunnar Myrdal: Social Engineering in the Modern World*, translated by Alex Skinner. Lanham, MA: Lexington Books.

Habel, Ylva (2002) *Modern Media, Modern Audiences: Mass Media and Social Engineering in the 1930s Swedish Welfare State.* Stockholm: Aura Förlag.

Hirdman, Yvonne (2002) *Alva Myrdal: Något kan man väl göra. Texter 1932–1984.* Stockholm: Carlsson Förlag.

Hirdman, Yvonne (2008) *Alva Myrdal: The Passionate Mind.* Bloomington: Indiana University Press.

Lindskog, Lars G. (1986) *Alva Myrdal: Förnuftet måste segra.* Stockholm: Sveriges Radios Förlag.

Myrdal, Alva and Myrdal, Gunnar (1935 [1934]) *Kris i befolkningsfrågan.* Folkupplaga. Tredje, Omarbetade Och Utvidgade Upplagan. Stockholm: Albert Bonniers Förlag.

Myrdal, Alva (1932) Kollektiv bostadsform [Collective housing'], in *Tiden* 24: 601–607.

Myrdal, A. (1933) Yrkeskvinnans barn [Working woman's children], in *Yrkeskvinnans klubbnytt* [*Working Women's Journal*], 63.

Myrdal, Alva (1934) Uppfostrad till "äkta quinnlighet". *Idun*, no. 8.

Myrdal, Alva (1941) *Nation and Family: The Swedish Experiment in Democratic Family and Population Policy.* New York: Harper.

Myrdal, Alva (1942) Kvinnovärde och kvinnokult. *Idun*, no. 23.

Runcis, Maija (1998) *Steriliseringar i folkhemmet.* Stockholm: Ordfront.

SOU (1999) Steriliseringsfrågor i Sverige 1935–1975 – Ekonomisk ersättning. SOU 1999:2.

SOU (2000) Steriliseringsfrågan i Sverige 1935–1975 – Historisk belysning – Kartläggning – Intervjuer jämte bilagor. SOU 2000:20.

Spektorowski, A. and Mizrachi, E. (2004) Eugenics and the welfare state in Sweden: The politics of social margins and the idea of a productive society. *Journal of Contemporary History* 39(3): 333–352.

Sydsvenskan (2003) 1600 tvångssteriliserade har fått skadestånd, 20 April. https://www.sydsvenskan.se/2003-04-20/1-600-tvangssteriliserade-har-fatt-skadestand.

5 Rosabeth Moss Kanter

Revolutionary roots and liberal spores

Deborah N. Brewis and Lara Pecis

Rosabeth Moss Kanter is a figure who looms large in organization studies. Since her first major projects in the 1970s, Kanter's ideas on leadership, change and power generated important shifts in thinking within the field at the time of their writing, and – perhaps most importantly – propagated many developments of management and organization research today. Her work is as expansive as it is rich in its theoretical and empirical contributions, ranging from communes to infrastructure; from leadership to strategy. In this chapter, we consider her contributions in two areas: by engaging with *Men and Women of the Corporation*[1] (first published in 1977) and *Change Masters: Innovations for Productivity in the American Corporation* (first published in 1983), we show how Kanter's early discussions on power, politics and exclusion represented important steps toward current discussions around inequalities at work, and towards understanding employees' empowerment for sustaining innovative organizations. Approaching Kanter's work through "zoom in, zoom out" (Kanter, 2011a), we synthesise and situate her ideas in relation to recent debates, arguing that they represented revolutionary shifts in thinking at the time of writing. Equally, we suggest that the works we examine feed into what might now be considered the liberal mainstream, and that scholars have, once more, seen the need for a critical shift in approaches to innovation and inequality.

Career and major works

Rosabeth Moss Kanter holds the Ernest L. Arbuckle Professorship at Harvard Business School and is a founding chair and director of the Harvard University Advanced Leadership Initiative. Her 1967 PhD, from the University of Michigan, led to her first two books, on communes, in 1972 and 1973, written while she was an associate professor at Brandeis University in Massachusetts. With an interim year teaching sociology at Harvard, Kanter stayed at Brandeis until 1977,[2] when, with partner Barry

A. Stein, she founded the consultancy Goodmeasure Inc. She also moved to Yale and published her book, *Men and Women of the Corporation*. This inspired the video *A Tale of 'O': On Being Different*,[3] which illustrates the core concepts of the book, and which has been used as a tool of diversity training. The ideas in this work have remained influential in the USA and beyond, informing organizational policies and practices around gender inequality in the workplace.

Kanter made a move to Harvard Business School in 1986 and has been a prolific writer on the topics of leadership, change and gender in the workplace. She is a regular contributor to the *Harvard Business Review*, which she edited from 1989 to 1992. Alongside her engagement with public and practitioner audiences throughout her career, in 1988 she advised presidential hopeful Michael Dukakis with whom she co-authored *Creating the Future: The Massachusetts Comeback and its Promise for America*, an account of the economic regeneration of the sitting governor's state and the role played by his leadership practices. Infrastructure is a continuing interest for Kanter and is the focus of her book *Move* (2015). Kanter became an established voice in the fields of change and innovation through works such as *The Change Masters: Innovations for Productivity in the American Corporation* (1983) and *When Giants Learn to Dance* (1989), seeking to understand how organizations can foster innovation and their capacity for change. Organizational change has been of interest since her earliest research on 19th-century and modern communes, in which she investigated their cohesiveness and longevity.

Kanter has received several honours for her work: from the Guggenheim Fellowship (1975) and the Wright Mills Award for *Men and Women of the Corporation*; to her induction into the Thinkers50 Hall of Fame[4]. Created by the Center for Families at Purdue University and the Center for Work and Family at Boston College, the *Rosabeth Moss Kanter Award* is now given in recognition of excellence in work–family research.

On inequality: the structural dynamics of power

In *Men and Women of the Corporation*, Kanter describes the dynamics of power in a multinational organization that she names "Indsco" – chosen not only for its size and influence in the USA but because of its claims to being "socially conscious". Kanter seeks to show the insidiousness of the relations that can shape opportunity and marginalisation. The work is rich with empirical examples that lend the work vibrancy and familiarity. The book has three objectives: the first is to chart the rise of the "administrative classes" in organizations, encompassing managerial and clerical roles; the second is to explore how certain roles shape possibilities for individual action, with reference to the manager, the secretary and the manager's wife; and the third is to understand how structures shape opportunity, power(lessness) and inequality.

Although Kanter describes it as a sub-theme, her work on gender was radical not only in its conceptualising of managers' wives as an oft-sidelined and important part of the organization, but also in its relational view of gender, understood to be a set of "images embedded in the roles [that] are inherent neither to the nature of the tasks themselves nor in the characteristics of the men and women; instead they are developed in response to the problems incumbents face in trying to live their organizational lives so as to maximise legitimacy or recognition of freedom" (1993: 5). This challenged existing discussions on whether gender differences were the root cause of people's differentiated behaviours within organizations (see for example in Sokolowska, 1965) and a source of inequality – positioning gender as an effect of organizing itself. This pivotal line of reasoning, that *roles create people*, has perhaps become one of Kanter's best-known contributions as a result of the third objective and final part of the book, which examines how the structure of hierarchies and the proportions of groups shape opportunities within organizations. Such structures, Kanter argues, are central to power: they can create virtuous cycles of opportunity and upward mobility, or present "a set of choices that are equally restricting, from which there is no escape" (Kanter, 1993: 11). Power, therefore, is understood as the capability "to get things done" (1993: 166), as finite and as (unequally) shared among organizational members. This view of power feeds into Kanter's conceptualisation of "empowerment" as "control over the conditions that make their actions possible" (1993: 166). Kanter is credited with being one of the first to popularise the notion, which is discussed in detail later on in this chapter.

We now delve into the book's discussions of gender inequality in the workplace. Given that Kanter's work brims with detail from her empirical setting, this close view illustrates how Kanter's perspective on the relation between structure and power becomes manifest in specific theoretical concepts.

Token women

Inspired by Simmel's studies of proportions and interpersonal dynamics, Kanter draws on her empirical data to suggest that "It was rarity and scarcity, rather than femaleness *per se*, that shaped the environment for women" (1993: 207). Kanter concentrates on the *skewed* group, where the ratio of one "type" of person to another is around 85 : 15. Those in the majority are "dominants", and those in the minority are "tokens". Elaborated in further work (1977), the effects of disproportionate representation are theorised as stemming from the heightened *visibility* of tokens; their small number means greater awareness and attention. This visibility leads to the intensification of performance pressures on token individuals. Kanter gives ethnographic accounts that describe how women at Indsco became symbolic – in their successes and failures, they were representative of all women in the dominant group, and examples to women lower down in the hierarchy. Whilst symbolic status meant that women gained some opportunities, the increased level of scrutiny meant that decisions which may seem of little importance, such as "what to wear and who to sit with at lunch" (1993: 215), took on significance for the individual and their type: "they are watching me [...] they are expecting me to prove something one way or the other" (1993: 216). This awareness by token women that they are the object of the (male) gaze (Mulvey, 1989) means that they are compelled to turn it upon themselves in self-regulation. Lewis and Simpson (2012) read visibility as a panoptic form of power that disciplines women as subjects; shaping who they can legitimately be. In response to performance pressures, Kanter argues that tokens might seek to outperform others and/or trade on their difference as a point of value; alternatively, they might seek to limit their visibility by adopting traits of the dominants, or avoiding conflict. Where reflecting the dominant group may be advantageous in some respects, women and their acceptability are still read by others in relation to their bodies: the "double bind" has since become an important idea in research on gender inequality, "where women who are considered feminine will be judged incompetent and women who are competent unfeminine" (Powell et al., 2009: 415). Ahmed talks about the dangers of visibility and conflict for people from marginalised groups: "When we give problems their names we can become a problem for those who do not want to register that there is a problem [...] You can become a problem by naming a problem". (2015: 9).

At the same time, *assimilation* occurs, whereby tokens are subject to stereotyping: whilst highly visible, tokens are not seen for their individuality. They are also subject to *role encapsulation/entrapment*, whereby there are a limited number of roles that they are permitted to occupy: Kanter talks specifically about women's roles as "mother", "seductress", "iron maiden" and "pet" (1993: 233–236). One might say that these roles represent a restricted set of lenses through which women become legible in organizations. Kanter asserts that gender, the source of the women's tokenism, acts as a *master status* that modifies their work identities: either in cases of "mistaken identity" where Indsco women were taken for "secretaries [...] wives or mistresses" (Kanter, 1993: 231), or as a qualifier that becomes attached to their identities by hyphenation, such as "woman-engineer" (1977: 968). This again restricts the possible recognition of individuality but also the sense that they belong in the workplace. The alienation of this dynamic is stark if we consider Shore et al.'s (2011) proposal that the experience of both belongingness and uniqueness is a prerequisite for the achievement of inclusion within organizations.

Lastly, *polarisation* is described by Kanter as the phenomenon by which differences are exaggerated for both token and dominant groups. The presence of difference means heightened awareness of both the commonalities within the group and difference from the perceived interloper(s). *Boundary heightening* occurs between the two groups in response to a felt threat through attention to culture – where the underlying assumptions and rationalities of the way things are done are brought into question, or at least habitual modes of being are brought into relief: "ironically, tokens unlike people of their type represented in greater proportion, are thus instruments for under*lining* rather than under*mining* majority culture" (emphasis in original, 1993: 223). Kanter describes how performances of camaraderie and prowess by men were observed in groups where women were present but not in sufficient numbers to introduce a "hybrid of conversational themes" (Kanter, 1993: 223). Token women were subject to tests of loyalty toward the dominant group, or positioned as interruptions to processes that would otherwise be easier, quicker, smoother.

Leadership and gender

Kanter talks about the women of Indsco's overall preference for men as leaders and attributes this to a *preference for power* (1993: 197). Finding no substantive differences between women and men's leadership strategies of styles, Kanter theorises that the preference is informed by the access that men tended to have to opportunities and the logic of betting on a winner (Kanter, 1993: 200). A preference reinforced by the "mean and bossy woman" stereotype (1993: 201) suffered by women. Kanter argues that women may be more inclined to lead in ways that involve close supervision of their subordinates because they themselves are subject to scrutiny and transmit downwards the effects of their relative powerlessness. Ferguson found a tendency for those of "difference" to be awarded only those roles that are highly rule-governed; this "bureaucratic domination" may further heighten the surveillance of those from marginalised groups (1984: 107). Although Kanter asserts that "power begets power" (1993: 168), she speaks to the upward accumulation of opportunity that can be enjoyed by an individual. Lewis and Simpson perspicaciously re-read Kanter's work to see power as a vortex through which the "dominant centre of male management is preserved" and male privilege maintains its hegemony (2012: 148–149). Women at Indsco were less likely to have powerful alliances and performed additional labour in resisting benevolent sexism from those seeking to protect them by "encapsulating them in safe positions" (1993: 203). Kanter's ideas on leadership have been cited in discussions about homosocial reproduction and the effects of powerlessness in organizing (e.g. Pfeffer, 1992), and in relation to women's networks where women's connections appear more effective when they are task-related rather than social, since the latter risks reinforcing stereotypes (Ibarra, 1992: 441).

Kanter situates gender primarily as something that is contained in bodies and subject to distortion through overgeneralisation by others. What is missing from her analysis, and has been developed since, is a perspective on leadership as gendered. This connects with some critics who point out that power relations are enacted not only through relative numbers, but also in the value that is placed on masculine attributes and male bodies. With regards to the former, scholars have found women leaders to be judged less favourably in terms of their congruity with leadership roles, and when "the prescriptions of a leader role [are] enacted by a woman" (Eagly and Karau, 2002: 573). Yoder and Sinnett (1985) and Heikes (1991) find that men do not experience the same effects when they are tokens in a group, but that sociocultural factors interact with proportions, pointing to the need to examine both structural and institutional dominance (Izraeli, 1983). With regards to the latter, the ideal worker is traditionally disembodied and the organization appears neutrally structured based on this assumption (Acker, 1990). This neutrality is disturbed by the presence of women's bodies that are less easily contained: they "intrude" into the workplace through menstruation, menopause and breastfeeding (Brewis and Sinclair 2000, Sayers and Jones, 2015). Compared with the supposed invisibility of men's bodies (Liu 2017), women are problematic. Knights (2015) argues that the embodied dimension of organizing needs recognition, and, to achieve this, the binary of masculine–feminine or male–female needs to be dismantled. This would afford us the capacity to relate to one another with a corporeal ethics (Pullen and Rhodes, 2014) that resists the oppression and denial of difference. In these ways, *Men and Women of the Corporation* lacks a political perspective on power that fully recognises how the exclusion of women involves struggle over meaning and value.

On the human side of innovation: people as agents of change

> Thus, individuals actually need to count for more, because it is people within the organization who come up with new ideas, who develop creative responses, and who push for change.
>
> (Kanter, 1983: 18)

The Change Masters: Innovations for Productivity in the American Corporation explores how corporate entrepreneurs – so-called "change masters" – envision productive change within the organization. In this book, Kanter examines 115 innovations in 10 high-tech companies, focusing on change and its enabling conditions. The study came at a turbulent time for the US economy: high bankruptcy rates, fierce competition from Japan and a high trade deficit. A pressing need for innovation in spite of social and economic challenges revealed that past practices were insufficient in a global market.

Kanter's analysis presents a striking finding for the time: companies that were progressive in their human resource practices had a significantly higher long-term profitability and financial growth than other companies (1983: 19). Such companies encouraged people at all levels to participate in suggesting new ideas and solving problems, and to engage in entrepreneurial activities. The companies that had integrative structures and organizational cultures of collaboration, teamwork, pride and commitment were the most successful. On the contrary, territorial protection and fighting across groups of bureaucratic organizations produced an illusion of managers' unilateral power. The book has a persuasive tone and calls for a "renaissance" of the corporation: to be innovative, companies would need to flatten hierarchies, decentralise power and nurture achievements.

Innovation and empowerment: troubling the mainstream

The Change Masters has influenced innovation research in at least three ways. First, *innovation as associated to change*. In Kanterian terms, innovation is the process of creating new ideas and problem-solving so that organizations can adapt. This idea is central to Kanter's work and is embedded in contemporary organizational analyses of innovation (Garud, Tuertscher and Van de Ven, 2013). Second, *innovation is a networked phenomenon*: the involvement of those at the grassroots level and a climate of innovation across the entire organization are preconditions of change. Stakeholders and constituencies outside the organization also stimulate change. Innovation, seen as a networked phenomenon, has since been widely investigated: for example, Hargadon (2003) outlines how breakthrough innovations often derive from a broad network of resources. This shifts the view of change masters from lone initiators of change to beneficiaries of growing webs of infrastructures, institutions, people and objects (see also Garud, Tuertscher and Van de Ven, 2013). Recent innovation research has recognised the role of technologies, objects, people, institutions and regulations in shaping the innovation journey (Geels, 2004; Garud and Rappa, 1994).

This has accompanied a perspective on *innovation as process* rather than as outcome. Going beyond the variance approach, Garud, Berends and Tuertscher (2017) outline three ways of understanding innovation as process that unfold on a spectrum ranging from process as "observed" (by the researcher looking for patterns of change) to process as "experienced" by its participatns (also, Garud 2008; Deken et al., 2016).

Kanter's work connects the human side of innovation and the structural conditions enabling it. In this sense, her work seems to lean towards "variance" approaches to innovation, which identify causality between independent and dependent variables that determine change (e.g. Brown and Eisenhardt, 1997). However, Kanter also brought *people* to the foreground at a time when attention to variance analyses of innovation dominated. Her writing, despite describing culture as a variable for change, attends to human endeavour: *The Change Masters* alternates Kanter's voice with those who have helped or hindered innovation in their organizations. "Empowerment" is understood to be the ability to invest in people, to enable them to have control over their work and to find ways for contributing to the organization. For Kanter, power is not diffused downwards from the top, but entails individuals seeking the means to explore and enthuse others' propensity for change. Power is sustained by access to support (endorsement, backing, approval and legitimacy), information (data, technical knowledge, expertise and political intelligence) and resources (funds, materials, time and space) (Kanter, 1982 and 1983). In integrative organizations, corporate entrepreneurs work in teams to produce small changes that lead, in turn, to wider impact. Empowerment, in *The Change Masters*, compels the reader to think beyond the limits of one's role, to embrace democratic approaches and to experiment. It does so by proposing practical responses to conduct that stifles innovation: the neglect of ideas from the grassroots, bureaucratic procedures, lack of collaboration, a fear-based work environment, discouragement, tight control, secrecy in decision-making, lack of transparency, focus on cuts and savings and assumptions of senior-management superiority. Some circumstances might require unilateral and authoritative decisions rather than collaborative efforts, for example when quick decisions are needed, but nevertheless, these "dilemmas of participation" can be managed, especially when they concern the inner workings of teams, teams' relations with the wider organization and evaluation of the process by onlookers and members alike. Kanter's concept of empowerment has been taken up within the psychology literature as a condition that might affect employees' powerlessness (Conger and Kanungo, 1988), and as a requisite for people to embrace responsibilities and express their creative energies (Spreizer, 1995).

Change management

In the final part of *The Change Masters*, Kanter explores five forces for change. First, Kanter introduces the idea of *departure from tradition*, which describes how organizations deviate from expectations, necessitating both flexibility and the deliberate creation of spaces for experimentation. The second force is a *galvanising event* that may occur outside the organization and its operating frameworks. Third, change requires strategic decisions to be made in conscious articulations of a direction, thus creating a *vision for the future*. Fourth, opportunities for change might drift away in the absence of an *individual prime mover*, that is, someone who takes the responsibility to activate change. Fifth and last, Kanter asserts that change would not be possible without the expression of *mechanisms* for new forms of action.

Kanter develops a systematic discussion of these forces in *Challenge of Organizational Change: How companies experience it and leaders guide it* (Kanter, Stein and Jick, 1992). In doing so, she develops a Big Three model of change, based on *movement, form* and *roles*. Kanter's understanding of change challenges Lewin's three-stage model linear and static approach. Yet, it seems that her own elaboration of change suffers from the widespread academic tendency to reduce change to its outcomes (e.g. Van de Ven, 1987; Pettigrew, 1987). This, Chia (1999) argues, is traceable to its intellectual roots of western civilization, ingrained in a metaphysics of substance that also led to the dominance of Newtonian physics. Kanter's use of typologies, hierarchies, systems and structures and other taxonomic classifications in the analysis of organizational change has also been criticised for its abstraction and for rendering fixed a continually transforming social reality (Chia, 1999). Despite explaining change in terms of dominant static categories, Kanter's work has allowed academics and practitioners to understand the importance of structure and individual actions in shaping stability and instability.

The disruptive force of Kanter's work resides in questioning traditional ways of managing, and in suggesting a new perspective on innovation that places central value on the human (Kanter, 2006). Her work implies that innovative companies that have integrative thinking can challenge established practices and be diverse and inclusive (Kanter, 1983), and that a corporate culture of relieving potential innovators from the bureaucratic structures that limit the expansion of their ideas will allow those ideas to flow down and up the pyramid (Kanter, 2006). Thirty-five years after her groundbreaking book on change masters, flexibility and openness to new ideas, a non-silo mentality and an emphasis on the human side of innovation remain key elements in the way management scholars think about innovation. Kanter continues to develop these ideas, suggesting more recently that companies should increase investment in employee empowerment and in emotional engagement with them to foster innovation (Kanter, 2011b).

For Kanter, successful organizations are social institutions; they stimulate internal collaboration and innovation through a coherent identity that is based on common values, meaning and purpose (2011b); and empowerment of employees through a strong organizational culture led by values and principles (Kanter, in Bernhut, 2009). Yet, the idea that employees' actions may be guided by their values and emotions has a normative implication that seems at odds with her transformative project. Kanter admits her notion of empowerment might challenge those on both sides of the aisle:

> I know that this may sound utopian to conservatives and exploitative to radicals. But my response is the same to critics of both ends of the political spectrum. It appears that when it is in the interests of the people involved, and they are given genuine opportunity and power, they can be committed to finding the time to contribute to solving organizational problems.
>
> (Kanter, 1983: 202)

Where next for promoting innovation and equality? Progress and barriers to change

> I had a mission to explain people's experience in such a way that they could both understand why it was happening to them, see the barriers, and then break through them.
>
> (Kanter, in Puffer, 2004: 97)

Having looked at some of Kanter's key contributions to the fields of inequality and innovation, we bring them together to examine approaches that have been taken to change organizations with respect to promoting gender equality and innovation. Both *Men and Women of the Corporation* and *Change Masters* opened the way for an understanding of equality, diversity and inclusion through their analysis of gender dynamics, the mechanisms of information transfer, cognitive biases and struggles for power. Kanter's concepts help us to see how such dynamics result in access to opportunities, resources and status; and for organizations as a whole in their capacity to change, innovate and be mobile (Ibarra, 2004). Bringing this chapter to a close, we take a look at the progress we have seen in the empowerment of those marginalised and of those attempting to innovate.

For marginalised groups, in Kanterian terms, we have seen changes with regards to an increase in the number of women in board-level positions, and in some industries and in countries where there have been mandatory or voluntary quotas for appointments. However, policies that attempt to stamp out discrimination and promote diversity have been critiqued as ineffective (Ahmed, 2007, Hoque and Noon, 2004), and attempts to intervene as overly individualised (Brewis, 2017, Brewis, 2019, Özbilgin and Tatli, 2011) or as reproducing gender stereotypes (Due Billing and Alvesson, 2000). In the digital sphere, which promises reduced visibility of gender for entrepreneurs, inequalities are seemingly reproduced through intersectional dynamics of difference (Dy et al., 2017). Kanter's work has perhaps underestimated patriarchal relations with regards to the backlash from dominant groups that attempts at change have received. Zimmer (1988) argues that Kanter's work on proportional dynamics has been used to sideline the issue of sexism in the workplace and wider society. Thus, we need to consider what it is that marginalised people are being *included in*.

The way in which we understand structure and its importance to reproducing inequalities has, as one would expect, moved forward since Kanter's writings. The use of typologies, hierarchies, systems and structures for understanding innovation and organizational change has moved from a reductionist approach toward the flux of social reality (Chia, 1999), emphasising heterogeneity, indeterminacy and surprise in organizational life. Innovation has been argued to be a process of human endeavour and experience (Garud, Berends and Tuertscher, 2017). Much like Kanter's take on leadership, what is perhaps missing from her analysis is a perspective of innovation *as gendered*. The ideal innovator has traditionally been disembodied and gender-neutral, something disturbed by the presence of women in the innovation process (Pecis, 2016). *The Change Masters* thus lacks politicisation of the micro-dynamics of participants of organizational changes and innovation, and the gendered practices sustaining them.

Conclusion

Despite the breadth of Kanter's influence in several areas of management and organization studies, we have found that her work is often reduced to a handful of ideas. Revisiting Kanter, it is easy to see how this might have come to be – her works are dense with empirical examples and theorisation, and her writing an unusual combination of lush ethnographic accounts and pragmatic typologies. Childs and Krook (2008) argue that one key idea in Kanter's work – that group dynamics are a consequence rather than a cause of proportional structuring – has suffered from reductionism itself in how it has been taken up in some research. The phenomenon of "critical mass theory" illustrates how the nuances of Kanter's hypotheses – in this case, about the factors that might affect group dynamics as they change from skewed to tilted or balanced – have been lost in contemporary literature (e.g. Joecks et al., 2013, Stichman et al., 2010).

Despite reductionist tendencies in how it has been taken up, Kanter's research on women in corporations, change and innovation was groundbreaking. On gender, Kanter's shift from thinking of women's inequalities as a problem of women's career choices and behaviour to a problem of structure within groups marked the assumption of gender differences as something actively reproduced and reinforced in organizational literature, and oppressive. This emphasis on structural inequalities encouraged women to lobby for interventions to reduce proportional inequality, and for supporting policies. These were a spectrum from liberal to radical actions: from women's networks and acceleration programmes to quotas for women at particular levels of seniority or in particular industries. Yet, in the context of current discussions about organizing difference, Kanter's work now seems to lack sufficient complexity in its capacity to address multiplicity. First, we need to account for multiplicity in difference: intersectionality theory asserts that socially produced categories of difference such as gender, class, disability and race are interconnected in the process of social exclusion (Crenshaw, 1997). Scholars have begun to show how intersecting differences inform the dynamics of privilege and oppression (Bell and Nkomo, 2001, Ruiz-Castro and Holvino, 2016). Second, we need to account for increased multiplicity in our understanding of gender. Although not explicitly acknowledged, Kanter's descriptions of camaraderie displays among men and heightening of "feminine" behaviours among women in response to role entrapment imply that gender is shaped by one's relations to others and also informs those relations. The performative view of gender (Butler, 1988, 1990, West and Zimmerman, 1987) has transformed the ways in which we understand gender as a phenomenon (see discussions in relation to the workplace – Benschop, 2017, Priola, 2007, Tyler and Cohen, 2010). We need to consider what Kanter's concepts might mean for Trans identities, non-binary genders and fluid genders. We suggest that her work might fruitfully be re-read with performativity, fluidity and/or greater multiplicity of gender in mind. Finally, the revolutionary aspiration in Kanter's work also echoes in the analysis of innovation and organizational change. Kanter highlighted the inevitable need to enact a culture for innovation that not only engages with the flattening of hierarchies, with organizational flexibility and with the creation of opportunities for employees to conduct meaningful work, but that is also more inclusive. Thus, for Kanter, empowering people in the organization is central to dismantling (gender) inequalities at work, and in the production of successful and innovative organizations.

Notes

1 Appearing in rankings of popular and influential books in organization studies.
2 https://www.britannica.com/biography/Rosabeth-Moss-Kanter
3 https://www.amazon.co.uk/tale-being-different-organization-Colophon/dp/0060907290#customerReviews
4 http://thinkers50.com/hall-of-fame/

Further reading

Original text by Kanter

Kanter, R.M. (1993). *Men and Women of the Corporation*, 2nd edn. New York: Basic Books.
Kanter, R.M. (1983). *The Change Masters: Corporate Entrepreneurs at Work*. New York: Touchstone Books.

Key academic text

Puffer, S.M. (2004). Introduction: Rosabeth Moss Kanter's men and women of the corporation and the change masters. *The Academy of Management Executive*, 18(2), 92–95.

Accessible resource

Kanter, R.M. (1977). Some effects of proportions on group life: Skewed sex ratios and responses to token women. *American Journal of Sociology*, 82(5), 965–990.
Kanter, R.M. (1988). When a thousand flowers bloom: Structural, collective and social conditions for innovation in organisation. In *Research in Organisational Behaviour*, edited by B.M. Staw and L.L. Cummings. Greenwich, CT: JAI Press.

References

Acker, J. (1990). Hierarchies, jobs, bodies: A theory of gendered organizations. *Gender & Society*, 4(2), 139–158.
Ahmed, S. (2007). "You end up doing the document rather than doing the doing": Diversity, race equality and the politics of documentation. *Ethnic and Racial Studies*, 30(4), 590–609.
Ahmed, S. (2015). Introduction: Sexism–A problem with a name. *New Formations: A Journal of Culture/Theory/Politics*, 86(1), 5–13.
Bell, E. and Nkomo, S.M. (2001). *Our Separate Ways*. Boston: Harvard Business Review Press.
Benschop, Y. (2017). *Multiple Femininities in Leadership?* Gendered Inclusion Seminar Series, Cranfield University, 23 October.

Bernhut, S. (2009). Supercorp: An interview with Rosabeth Moss Kanter. *Ivey Business Journal (Online)*, London (September/October).

Brewis, D.N. (2017). Social justice "lite"? Using emotion for moral reasoning in diversity practice. *Gender, Work & Organization*, 24(5), 519–532.

Brewis, D.N. (2018). Duality and fallibility in practices of the self: The "inclusive subject" in diversity training. *Organization Studies*, 40(1), 93–114.

Brewis, J. and Sinclair, J. (2000). 10 Exploring embodiment: Women, biology and work. In Hassard, J., Holliday, R. and Willmott, H. (Eds.) *Body and Organization*. London: Sage, pp. 192–214.

Brown, S.L. and Eisenhardt, K.M. (1997). The art of continuous change: Linking complexity theory and time-paced evolution in relentlessly shifting organizations. *Administrative Science Quarterly*, 42(1), 1–34.

Butler, J. (1988). Performative acts and gender constitution: An essay in phenomenology and feminist theory. *Theatre Journal*, 40(4), 519–531.

Butler, J. (1990). *Gender Trouble. Feminism and the Subversion of Identity*. New York and London: Routledge.

Chia, R. (1999). A "rhizomic" model of organizational change and transformation: Perspective from a metaphysics of change. *British Journal of Management*, 10(3), 209–227.

Childs, S. and Krook, M.L. (2008). Critical mass theory and women's political representation. *Political Studies*, 56(3), 725–736.

Crenshaw, K. (1997). Intersectionality and identity politics: Learning from violence against women of colour. In Shanley, M.L. and Narayan, U. (Eds.), *Reconstructing Political Theory*. Oxford: Polity Press, pp. 178–193.

Conger, J.A. and Kanungo, R.N. (1988). The empowerment process: Integrating theory and practice. *Academy of Management Review*, 13(3), 471.

Deken, F., Carlile, P.R., Berends, H. and Lauche, K. (2016). Generating novelty through interdependent routines: A process model of routine work. *Organization Science*, 27(3), 659–677.

Dy, A.M., Marlow, S. and Martin, L. (2017). A web of opportunity or the same old story? Women digital entrepreneurs and intersectionality theory. *Human Relations*, 70(3), 286–311.

Due Billing, Y. and Alvesson, M. (2000). Questioning the notion of feminine leadership: A critical perspective on the gender labelling of leadership. *Gender, Work & Organization*, 7, 144–157.

Eagly, A.H. and Karau, S.J. (2002). Role congruity theory of prejudice toward female leaders. *Psychological Review*, 109(3), 573.

Ferguson, K.E. (1984). *The Feminist Case against Bureaucracy* (Vol. 104). Philadelphia: Temple University Press.

Garud, R. (2008). Conferences as venues for the configuration of emerging organizational fields: The case of cochlear implants. *Journal of Management Studies*, 45(6), 1061–1088.

Garud, R. and Rappa, M.A. (1994). A socio-cognitive model of technology evolution: The case of cochlear implants. *Organization Science*, 5(3), 344–362.

Garud, R., Berends, H. and Tuertscher, P. (2017). 15 Qualitative approaches for studying innovation as process. In Mir, R. and Jain, S. (Eds.), *The Routledge*

Companion to Qualitative Research in Organization Studies. New York and Oxon: Routledge, pp. 226–247.

Garud, R., Tuertscher, P. and Van de Ven, A.H. (2013). Perspectives on innovation processes. *Academy of Management Annals*, 7(1), 775–819.

Geels, F.W. (2004). From sectoral systems of innovation to socio-technical systems: Insights about dynamics and change from sociology and institutional theory. *Research Policy*, 33(6), 897–920.

Hargadon, A. (2003). *How Breakthroughs Happen: The Surprising Truth about How Companies Innovate*. Boston: Harvard Business Press.

Heikes, E.J. (1991). When men are the minority: The case of men in nursing. *The Sociological Quarterly*, 32(3), 389–401.

Hoque, K. and Noon, M. (2004). Equal opportunities policy and practice in Britain: evaluating the "empty shell" hypothesis. *Work, Employment and Society*, 18(3), 481–506.

Ibarra, H. (1992). Homophily and differential returns: Sex differences in network structure and access in an advertising firm. *Administrative Science Quarterly*, 37(3), 422–447.

Ibarra, H. (2004). Men and women of the corporation and the change masters: Practical theories for changing times. *The Academy of Management Executive*, 18(2), 108–111.

Izraeli, D.N. (1983). Sex effects or structural effects? An empirical test of Kanter's theory of proportions. *Social Forces*, 62(1), 153–165.

Joecks, J., Pull, K. and Vetter, K. (2013). Gender diversity in the boardroom and firm performance: What exactly constitutes a "critical mass?". *Journal of Business Ethics*, 118(1), 61–72.

Kanter, R.M. (1982). The middle manager as innovator. *Harvard Business Review*, 60(4), 95–105.

Kanter, R.M. (2006). Innovation: The classic traps. *Harvard Business Review*, 84(11), 72–83.

Kanter, R.M. (2011a). Zoom in, zoom out. *Harvard Business Review*, 89(3), 112–116.

Kanter, R.M. (2011b). How great companies think differently. *Harvard Business Review*, 89(11), 66–78.

Kanter, R.M., Stein, B. and Jick, T.D. (1992). *The Challenge of Organizational Change: How Companies Experience It and Leaders Guide It*. New York: Free Press.

Knights, D. (2015). Binaries need to shatter for bodies to matter: Do disembodied masculinities undermine organizational ethics? *Organization*, 22(2), 200–216.

Lewis, P. and Simpson, R. (2012). Kanter revisited: Gender, power and (in)visibility. *International Journal of Management Reviews*, 14(2), 141–158.

Liu, H. (2017). The masculinisation of ethical leadership dis/embodiment. *Journal of Business Ethics*, 144(2), 263–278.

Mulvey, L. (1989). Visual pleasure and narrative cinema. In *Visual and Other Pleasures, Language, Discourse, Society*. London: Palgrave Macmillan, pp. 14–26.

Özbilgin, M. and Tatli, A. (2011). Mapping out the field of equality and diversity: Rise of individualism and voluntarism. *Human Relations*, 64(9), 1229–1253.

Pecis, L. (2016). Doing and undoing gender in innovation: Femininities and masculinities in innovation processes. *Human Relations*, 69(11), 2117–2140.

Pettigrew, A.M. (1987). *The Management of Strategic Change*. Oxford: Basil Blackwell.

Pfeffer, J. (1992). *Managing with Power: Politics and Influence in Organizations*. Brighton, MA: Harvard Business Press.

Powell, A., Bagilhole, B. and Dainty, A. (2009). How women engineers do and undo gender: Consequences for gender equality. *Gender, Work & Organization*, 16(4), 411–428.

Priola, V. (2007). Being female doing gender. Narratives of women in education management. *Gender and Education*, 19(1), 21–40.

Puffer, S.M. (2004). Changing organizational structures: An interview with Rosabeth Moss Kanter. *The Academy of Management Executive*, 18(2), 96–105.

Pullen, A. and Rhodes, C. (2014). Corporeal ethics and the politics of resistance in organizations. *Organization*, 21(6), 782–796.

Ruiz Castro, M. and Holvino, E. (2016). Applying intersectionality in organizations: Inequality markers, cultural scripts and advancement practices in a professional service firm. *Gender, Work & Organization*, 23(3), 328–347.

Sayers, J.G. and Jones, D. (2015). Truth scribbled in blood: Women's work, menstruation and poetry. *Gender, Work & Organization*, 22(2), 94–111.

Shore, L.M., Randel, A.E., Chung, B.G., Dean, M.A., Holcombe Ehrhart, K. and Singh, G. (2011). Inclusion and diversity in work groups: A review and model for future research. *Journal of Management*, 37(4), 1262–1289.

Sokolowska, M. (1965). Some reflections on the different attitudes of men and women towards work. *International Labour Review*, 92, 35.

Spreitzer, G.M. (1995). Psychological empowerment in the workplace: Dimensions, measurement, and validation. *Academy of Management Journal*, 38(5), 1442–1465.

Stichman, A.J., Hassell, K.D. and Archbold, C.A. (2010). Strength in numbers? A test of Kanter's theory of tokenism. *Journal of Criminal Justice*, 38(4), 633–639.

Tyler, M. and Cohen, L. (2010). Spaces that matter: Gender performativity and organizational space. *Organization Studies*, 31(2), 175–198.

Van de Ven, A.H. (1987). *Review Essay: Four Requirements for Processual Analysis, The Management of Strategic Change*. Oxford: Blackwell, 330–341.

West, C. and Zimmerman, D.H. (1987). Doing Gender. *Gender & Society*, 1(2), 125–151.

Yoder, J.D. and Sinnett, L.M. (1985). Is it all in the numbers? A case study of tokenism. *Psychology of Women Quarterly*, 9(3), 413–418.

Zimmer, L. (1988). Tokenism and women in the workplace: The limits of gender-neutral theory. *Social Problems*, 35(1), 64–77.

6 The organizational condition
Hannah Arendt and the radical domestication of freedom

Peter Bloom

Hannah Arendt was one of the foremost intellectuals of the 20th century. She was at once a philosopher, social theorist and public intellectual, and her thinking redefined historical and contemporaneous understandings of politics, economy and culture. Arendt was particularly renowned for her examination and challenging of sovereign power, broadly defined as the political governance of individuals and communities by a ruler. Her insights, furthermore, remain eminently relevant today. Indeed, Arendt's interrogation of the origins and mechanics of totalitarianism, or the attempt to establish "total control" by political rulers over a population, are especially timely in an era that is witnessing the potential resurgence of authoritarianism and quite xenophobic right-wing populism globally. This is perhaps especially true in this climate of neoliberalism in which all spheres of life are being increasingly made to conform to values of efficiency, productivity and profitability associated with the free market. Further, her philosophical intervention in the areas of thinking, willing and judging (especially associated with Kant) are arguably timeless in their import.

Nevertheless, there is comparatively little use of her theories within organizations studies (see for instance Vino, 1996). This lack is particularly surprising given that her distinguishing of "labour", "work" and "action" as well as her emphasis on the importance of natality are quite relevant to contemporary discussions of organizational life and politics within the field. Significantly, Arendt offers a sustained critique of sovereign power that resonates with critical organizational scholarship, which is concerned with how to challenge and transcend traditional and patriarchal forms of governance linked to values of control and regulation.

Yet Arendt's contributions to organization studies specifically and contemporary politics generally are arguably much more fundamental. Her theories reveal organizing as foundational to the human condition itself – vital to the very activity of being human. Further, Arendt provides a novel and non-essentialist perspective of alienation, one that is as relevant to mass society as it is to daily organizational reality. From this basis, Arendt offers a fresh critique of neoliberalism as an alienating force that exchanges freedom and natality for management and entrepreneurial innovation. However, perhaps her most important contribution is allowing us to reconsider and re-enact a radical form of organization that replaces patriarchal and sovereign forms of rule for one in which we individually and collectively create new ways of "being at home" in the world.

This chapter investigates, therefore, how Arendt's insights provide a philosophical basis for critically reflecting on the relation between organization and power. Notably, it draws on her ideas linked to "vita activa" (e.g. the active life) for radically reconfiguring the very basis of organizational politics. It begins by highlighting the significance of "organizing" for her notion of the "human condition" encompassing the activities of "labour", "work" and "action". It will then draw on this discussion to connect her ideas of "worldly alienation" to current experiences of organizational disenchantment. This broader critique will be followed by a more focused analysis of how these insights on alienation lend themselves to a deeper challenging of neoliberalism with its attempt to displace "vita activa" with "vita management". It will conclude with a deeper exploration of the role of Arendt's theories of "home" and "interval time" in informing a contemporary radical organizational politics and "life".

Organizing the human condition

Hannah Arendt wrote perhaps the definitive book on "the human condition". In her arguably masterwork of the same title, Arendt theoretically and historically traces out what it means to be human. In particular, using the classical Greeks as her model, she distinguishes between the activities of "labour", "work" and "action" – in so doing challenging both Liberal and Marxian accounts and creating an entirely fresh perspective for approaching individual development and social relations. She also offers an alternative normative lens from which to consider abiding questions of morality and politics – questions that can simultaneously inform and be expanded by organization studies thinking.

Critically, Arendt focuses her attention not on conventional questions of human nature or the determinates of human history, but rather on contrasting modes of living. Arendt distinguished "vita activa" from "vita contemplativa". The former represents the sphere of human activity while the latter represent mental reflection. Significantly, Arendt does not explicitly prioritise one over the other. Instead, she critically reflects on how their dynamics shapes human experience generally. More to the point, Arendt is concerned that philosophy and history are too often more concerned with what people thought than with the forms and spheres of activities that conditioned their shared existence. According to Canovan (1994: 101), one of the foremost scholarly interpreters of Arendt,

> The first point to bear in mind is that Arendt herself did not regard *The Human Condition* as the definitive statement of her political theory, but rather as a kind of preliminary to political theory proper, an investigation of the human activities that have the most bearing upon politics and have been the most misunderstood.

Specifically, Arendt distinguished three categories of activities central to the "human condition". The first is that of "labour", which denotes the processes and actions necessary for the material reproduction of life. Arendt describes it as "the activity which corresponds to the biological process of the human body" (Arendt, 1958: 7). Here, the emphasis is on the natural elements and rhythms that allow for humanity's continued survival and proliferation. Quoting Vino (1996: 311), in this regard,

> Labour takes place within the private sphere and it is the realm of necessity. It can only be defined in the negative as an incessant consumption of energy, shaped by the need for subsistence and securing the objects of the world we live in. It is a struggle against the continuous and unstoppable decay of things; against the disorder always lurking in the world.

The second fundamental activity Arendt proposes is that of "work". Unlike "labour", it refers to the unnatural parts of life, those elements that we produce and are durable. It connotes the broader world that humans create and inhabit as well as the cultural artifacts that come to define our lives. It is, hence, associated with values of "worldliness", as it is outwardly oriented in so much as it speaks to an unnatural but all-pervasive social existence. Arendt declares thus that

> The things of the world have the function of stabilising human life and their objectivity resides in the fact [...] that men, their ever-changing nature notwithstanding, can retrieve their sameness, that is their identity by being related to the same chair and the same table. In other words, against the subjectivity of men stands the objectivity of the man-made world rather than the sublime indifference of an untouched nature.
>
> (Arendt, 1958: 137)

The final, but by no means any less significant, activity is "action". It profoundly differs from both "labour" and "work" in that it exists solely between humans "without the intermediary of things or matter" (Ibid: 7).

Further, unlike these preceding activities, it is premised on the individuality and difference of humans. "It corresponds", according to Arendt (Ibid: 7), "to the fact that men, not Man, live on earth. and inhabit this world". Importantly,

> Action would be an unnecessary luxury, a capricious interference with general laws of behaviour, if men were endlessly reproducible repetitions of this same model, whose essence or nature was the same for all and was as predictable as the nature or essence of any other thing. Plurality is the condition of human action because we are all the same, that is, human in such a way that nobody is ever the same as anyone who has ever lived, lives, or will live.
>
> (Ibid: 8)

Each of these activities, of course, goes beyond the individual (e.g. "the human") and toward a shared existence of humanity itself. The labour proscribed for individual survival encompasses the survival of the species as a whole. Work, conversely, provides humans with a sense of cultural longevity, a permanence that transcends their own lifetime. And it is through action, the expression of our individual uniqueness through our deeds, that our history is written and established.

Interestingly, Arendt only implicitly touches on the significance of organizations and organizing for "vita activa". This is mentioned more in passing than as an explicit object of study. Arendt describes the diverse ways in which individuals are organized, reflecting various manifestations of what it means to be human. Tellingly, Arendt rejects the basis of human organization on any essential nature or external authority. Rather, as political theorist Bonnie Honig (1991) argues, it was the actual performance of founding an institution collectively that served to legitimate and sustain institutions. Referring to the American Revolution and writing of the Declaration of Independence, Arendt (1965: 199) proclaims

> It was the authority which the act of foundation carried within itself, rather than the belief in an immortal Legislator, or the promises of reward and threats of punishment in a "future state", or even the doubtful self evidence of the truths enumerated in the preamble to the Declaration of Independence, that assured stability for the new republic.

Vino (1996) in particular explores the importance of Arendt for organization studies. He highlights the role of action for reconceiving politics – notably as a space for fostering radical natality in otherwise regulatory processes and values. He contends that action is special, not guided by necessity as is labour nor by usefulness as is work but by the ineluctable individuality of each of the social actors, it is also the activity through which men interact in a completely unpredictable manner. Not by accident, is the concept of action related to that of birth and beginning: just as birth means a new beginning, so action means the manifestation of a wondrous, highly unlikely event.

(312)

He politically augments this promotion of action with Arendt's notions of thinking, representing the human ability to produce and spread meaning. Within the context of organizations, action and thought combine to reconfigure institutional relations. Hence, in his view:

Action, the expression of the plurality of individuals present in an organization, with its irreducible unpredictability, is what characterizes "organizational life". This makes the polis metaphor a relevant instrument for understanding some aspects of organization politics. It stresses how power, necessary as it may be, needs legitimization, which is ultimately achieved through discursive practices. Organizational actors move in the field of the possible and not of the necessary. Understanding what occurs thus has to do with the search for meaning, rather than with the search for "rules of behavior". It requires, in other words, thinking and reflection.

(322)

This reading valuably shows the potential significance of Arendt in informing organizational politics. However, it is by no means exhaustive. Building and expanding on Vino, there emerges a perhaps even more fundamental way to use Arendt to concretely reconceptualise the relation of organizations and politics. Notably, it is how these activities of the human condition are socially organized that is politically crucial. The next section will explore, in particular, the alienation experienced when this activity of organization is taken away from humans.

From world to organizational alienation

Arendt's insights on the human condition critically shed light on the ways organizing is fundamental to the human condition. Importantly, Arendt was writing primarily in the backdrop of the devastating carnage of the Second World War. She was thus responding to the rise of totalitarianism, the almost inconceivable evil of the Holocaust and the emerging corporatisation of Western capitalist society. Her critique was consequently targeted at a social reality marked by conformism, bureaucracy and the nuclear threat of the Cold War (for a broader understanding of the present-day relevance of this period, see especially Cooke, 2006), and her insights contain much value for our present-day organizational condition – revealing how modern organizations restrict the ability of people to freely organize their work, life and actions.

For Arendt, a primary concern of the modern world was the collapse of the traditional public and private sphere and the rise of the all-encompassing social sphere in its place. Arendt describes the public sphere as the place of politics par excellence as it was the only space where humans were conventionally free from necessity. By contrast, the private sphere is what historically allowed for the public sphere, and hence politics, to exist, as it provided the domestic foundations for one to meet their biological needs. In the wake of the industrialised revolution, the public and private spheres essentially merged, according to Arendt, as the state became the primary provider for ensuring both material survival and political change. There was thus no realm where free action could exist, as all pluralism and individual deeds were directed within this new "social realm".

Notably, the latter completely rejected the sphere of human action for the security of regulation and a predictable future. Arendt observes in one of her seminal works, *On Violence*:

> Events, by definition, are occurrences that interrupt routine processes and routine procedures; only in a world where nothing of importance ever happens could the futurologists' dream come true. Predictions of the future are never anything but projections of present automatic processes and procedures, that is, of occurrences that are likely to come to pass if men do not act and if nothing unexpected happens; every action, for better or worse, and every accident necessarily destroys the whole pattern in whose frame the prediction moves and where it finds its evidence.
>
> (Arendt, 1970: 7)

A crucial aspect of action – and hence politics – is its spontaneity and unpredictability. Arendt introduces, according to Curthoys (2002: 49), a "public ethos, a disposition to communicate and deliberate rather than indoctrinate, to act spontaneously rather than surrender the language of politics to impersonal historical and material forces". The fear of this volatility is a universal feature of human society, witnessed historically in the diverse means through which individuals and groups trade the freedom of creating something new and surprising for the safety of established economic and cultural practices. In the 20th century, the introduction of "pseudo-science" to explain human affairs is borne out of a desire to do away with the fear of the unknown and the random that otherwise define human existence.

This complete socialisation of humanity was a direct threat to human freedom in a number of profound ways. At stake was the stripping of individuals of any agency to shape their destiny. History was reduced to predictable models and already determined trajectories. Here, events are replaced by probability, action by regulation. The potential for new beginnings is undermined by the need for institutionalisation and quantification. To this effect, Arendt rejects the "command–obedience" model of power that "equates power with the rule of law and presupposes that the paradigmatic power relation is that by which a sovereign imposes his will on his subjects" (Allen, 2002: 132).

Arendt condemns, therefore, modernity's "world alienation". The inability of humans to be free and become instead imprisoned by ideologies and industrialised processes. Arendt bemoans the rise of "mass society", with its emphasis on conformity and anonymity. This transforming of people into the "masses" prevents them from expressing their individual differences and from creating anything truly new through their uniqueness. Hence Arendt decries a politics based on sovereignty and thus obedience, declaring that "Politically, the identification of freedom with sovereignty is perhaps the most pernicious and dangerous consequence of the philosophical equation of freedom and free will. … If men wish to be free it is precisely sovereignty they must renounce" (Arendt, 1961: 164–165).

There is an important but implicit organizing dimension to this alienation. Specifically, our capacity as humans to organize how we live, work and act is crucial to our overall freedom. Tellingly, a key critique of Arendt – both in her own time and afterwards – applies to her strict separation between the public and private spheres as well as to her complete normative dismissal of the radical possibilities contained within the emergent social sphere (see Breen, 2007). These reflect a perhaps exaggerated emphasis on the classical politics of the Greek agora, where the private household was acknowledged as crucial but also secondary to the public sphere of politics between free men. In particular, the role that politics could play in transforming the private sphere, politicising that which was previously socialised.

A less explored but no less important critique is Arendt's lack of critical engagement with the radical political-role organizations. This, moreover, points to the modern alienation humans encounter within organizations. Organizational scholars have been at the forefront of such discussions. Namely, they have drawn on a diverse range of critical theoretical perspectives to critique processes of managerialism, work intensification and the evolving manifestations of organizational control in the context of late capitalism. Similarly to Arendt's, their critiques go beyond Marxian concerns of economic exploitation and toward employees' social and political disempowerment.

Absolutely crucial, in this regard, is the use of organizing to directly challenge organizational alienation. Dean (2016) speaks explicitly about the turning of the crowd into an organized political party that not only demands revolutionary change but also serves as a space for individual and collective experimentation for manifesting values of equality and free expression. This account challenges liberal autonomy for a comprehensive account of human agency – one located within organizations and achieved through organizing. In opposing modern forms of organizational control, and with them the demand for conformity, institutions evolve from sites of regularity and socialisation to places of action and politics. They also provide humans the opportunity to overcome their organizational alienation, concretely organizing their labour, work and actions in such a way as to increase their sense of security and freedom rather than exacerbate their material precarity and demands for obedience.

Just as significantly, this more critically orientated organizational perspective offers a critical lens for examining the changing character of this worldly and organizational alienation. Thus, traditional forms of organizational control have given way to new experiences of alienation associated with neoliberalism. As will be explored in greater depth in the next section, neoliberalism has restricted human activity to the narrow ideological limits of profitably managing our existence. Tellingly, this mode of being does not completely eschew the field of action and as such pluralism. Rather, it redirects it toward asserting our individuality within the confines of a competitive marketplace – whether in the economic, personal or political realms. Yet, it also points toward the possibility of creating a more empowering and liberating way for organizing the human condition.

Overcoming vita management

Arendt observes that a crucial inspiration for writing about the human condition was how uninspiring most found their current existence. Arendt (1963) describes the space race as a profound technological achievement built on human disappointment. Notably, it showed a desire to escape the planet and its social world. Here, blasting off into space represented a deep-seated earthly existential malaise.

Arendt connects this human disappointment to the global spread of capitalism. She despairs of the victory of "animal laborans" over "homo faber" – the triumph of labour over work. Traditionally, "homo faber" referred to the ability of people to use tools to shape their destiny and environment. Here, craftsmanship and creation are raised up to a specific human ability to change their lives and social reality. The world and our fate must be constantly worked upon and aided through the artificial invention of new tools and products. It was only through this experience of creation that individuals were able to produce a "shared world", and in doing so lay the foundations for action and with it politics and freedom. By contrast, "animal laborans" prioritised the production of humans as simple labouring commodities who created and consumed only impermanent mass-produced goods.

For Arendt, this was therefore the transformation of humanity into mere workers. She attributes this to the reconfiguration of the human condition around the goals of production and profit. Critically, Arendt observes that animal laborans has become the de facto universal modern human condition, pervading all areas of personal and social existence. It organizes, hence, our labour, work and action in line with industrialisation. In the present neoliberal era, the emphasis has again evolved from production to efficiency, from industrialisation to marketisation. It is therefore questionable the extent to which either homo faber or animal laborans still accurately reflects the 21st-century human condition. It is not so much work or tools that are prioritised, but entrepreneurship and fiscal acuity. Manufacturing our individual and collective destiny has surrendered to its profitable innovation and exploitation.

The emphasis has evolved from the proper bureaucratic organization of the human condition to its effective market management. More precisely, fundamental human activities must be continually successfully combined so that a person and society best maximise their market opportunities. Quoting Wendy Brown (2015: 17), this represents the transformation from "homo politicus" to "homo economicus" based on "the image of man as an entrepreneur of himself". Arendt warns, hence, that "neoliberal reason, ubiquitous today in statecraft and the workplace, in jurisprudence, education and culture, and a vast range of quotidian activity, is converting the distinctly political character, meaning and operation of democracy's constituent elements into economic ones". Autonomy and control are reduced to the free capability of individuals and organizations to optimise how they use their labour in a way that best takes advantage of a rapidly changing marketplace.

This is witnessed, for instance, in the cultural promotion of "work–life balance", in which the professional and personal must be integrated so that they become mutually reinforcing. In practice, this cultural ideal is often transformed into a demand to make one's life "work for you" – resulting in heightened work intensification and economic anxiety (see Bloom, 2016). More fundamentally,

> Corporate culturists commend and legitimise the development of a technology of cultural control that is intended to yoke the power of

self determination to the realization of corporate values from which employees are encouraged to derive a sense of autonomy and identity.

(Willmott, 1993: 563)

It also stands as a new paradigm for conceiving and enacting the human condition. If homo faber eschewed the worshipful person and society for the hardworking producer, and animal laborans worshipped the making and consuming of perishable goods, the neoliberal human is one that replaces these modes of being for one that promotes competition and market savvy. The new idol is that of the victorious CEO who combines vision and ruthlessness to beat out his or her rivals. All spheres of human existence are transformed into a competitive marketplace (Bloom and Rhodes, 2018). We must compete against each other for the next job, for the right partner, for the political party who will most benefit us.

This new management of the human condition is thus universal in scope and insatiable in its expansion. It is telling that a buzzword of the contemporary era is "boundaryless work" – meaning positively that people can have greater choice in changing careers and organizations. What is revealed though, critically, is how ideas of "employability" and the job demands have transcended the boundaries of the workplace and the conventional sphere of "work". They now encompass all aspects of a person's life and decision-making. Here, under neoliberalism, individuals are "simultaneously always a producer, always a family member and always a consumer" (Fleming and Spicer, 2004: 90).

Vita activa is now vita management in which activity is channelled toward and the possibility of action exchanged for the innovative and disciplining management of our labour, work and actions. Equally troubling is that there appears to be little possibility of escape from this neoliberal condition. It has infected all areas of our lives – from our material survival, to our cultural creations, to the ways we express our uniqueness in relation with one another. Arendt provides a critical perspective for comparing the general importance of organization for human activity to the present importance of management for shaping the contemporary human condition. Her insights, though, also reveal the radical political possibilities for changing this seemingly inescapable condition.

Radically domesticating organizations

Arendt is perhaps the rare theorist who puts forward a clear ideal toward which social relations should strive. However, her arguable idealisation of the Greek agora may seem rather irrelevant for the 21st century. In any case, as this chapter has sought to reveal, at the very least her ideas on alienation remain timely in the extreme. They reflect the neoliberal organization of the human condition to repress newness and freedom in the name of entrepreneurship and management. Nevertheless, her insights can also positively inform the radical organization of our contemporary world.

It is tempting to view Arendt's politics as ultimately anti-organizational. Arendt excoriates sovereignty because it seems to imply any attempt at institutionalisation as at best a necessary evil. As political theorist Annabel Herzog (2004: 20) presciently notes, Arendt's ultimate goal was the creation of a "worldwide anarchic (that is, based on no predetermined rule) politics of de-localization and re-localization; in her terms, a politics of free movement of founded identities, a cosmopolitanism, which, nevertheless, would have nothing to do with global sovereignty". Furthermore, her praise of the classical demos and implicit railing against social democracy or socialism as mere forms of modern "socialisation" would appear to place freedom at odds with any and all forms of governance or administration. Indeed, in her classic later work on "what is authority", Arendt maintains that while the loss of traditional authorities such as religion may be disorienting for modern subjects, the loss of such ontological security does not preclude the human ability for social creation. Quoting her at length:

> Authority, resting on a foundation in the past as its unshaken cornerstone, gave the world the permanence and durability which human beings need precisely because they are mortals – the most unstable and futile beings we know of. Its loss is tantamount to the loss of the groundwork of the world, which indeed since then has begun to shift, to change and transform itself with ever-increasing rapidity from one shape into another, as though we were living and struggling with a Protean universe where everything at any moment can become almost anything else. But the loss of worldly permanence and reliability – which politically is identical with the loss of authority – does not entail, at least not necessarily, the loss of the human capacity for building, preserving, and caring for a world that can survive us and remain a place fit to live in for those who come after us.
>
> (Arendt, 1961: 3)

Thus digging deeper, a dramatically different picture begins to emerge. Namely, Arendt appreciates the Greek polis not simply for its politics but for its attempt to organize the different activities of the human condition to allow for freedom as such. Put differently, while the private household and slave economy of Greece, in her view, should certainly be morally castigated, this ethical repulsion should not lead us to ignore the importance of considering human society as a whole that must be integrated in such a way as to permit people the time and space to engage in free action with each other. Canovan (1985) describes this as a politics that permits people to focus on what is traditionally considered "high culture". It was critical to not allow the needs of material reproduction and cultural production to overshadow and repress the opportunities for individuals to express their uniqueness and act in such a way that was not instrumentally driven toward a pre-conceived end.

There is, therefore, a quite radical economic agenda that can be drawn from Arendt. At the most basic level, Arendt shares prominent Marxist Rosa Luxemburg's fear that nationalism and imperialism lead inevitably to the industrialised "barbarity" of extermination camps (see Spencer, 2006). Yet Arendt also directly takes socialism and Communism to task for their similar emphasis on conformity at the expense of the individual freedom that she finds in capitalism (see Beiner, 1990). Through her embrace of the private household in Greece (for all its own classical barbarity), she reveals how essential it is that people gain freedom from the demands of labour if they are to be humanly free. In modern terms, this means that scarcity must be eliminated, for otherwise individuals will be unable to independently act or think. Interestingly, this elimination of scarcity as a pre-requisite for freedom is precisely the conclusion that Sartre would come to in his own theories of existentialism. Society, hence, must be organized to promote freedom, rather than detract from it.

This reading has clear implications for organizations themselves. The question is: how do you create the conditions for organizational politics? Importantly, the political, here, does not mean promoting one change agenda over another. Rather, it implies the exploration of different ways of being in the world based on our own personal uniqueness. It further focuses on actions that are not caught in a logic of means and ends but rather revel in the joy of simply acting to create the potential for something new to exist. Arendt (1965: 223; also see Markell, 2006) provocatively, observes "Perhaps the very fact that these two elements, the concern with stability and the spirit of the new, have become opposites in political thought and terminology … must be recognized to be among the symptoms of our loss".

Organizations must themselves be organized to allow such spaces for free action and expression to be manifested. This means challenging cultures that rely upon ideas of scarcity, fear and lack to pressure individuals into institutional obedience. It also demands moving away from simplistic "us vs. them" conflictual notions of organizational life. Instead, it involves creating institutions and institutional relations that promote "free participation" and the multiplicity of identities as well as tensions experienced by organizational subjects. Olson (1997: 461), hence, draws on the anarchist collectives founded during the Spanish civil war to highlight "the practical aspects of establishing and maintaining the federated council system capable of maintaining a highly participatory and hence truly democratic society".

At stake is the creation of a new sense of worldly and organizational temporality. Arendt, in her later works, argues for what she terms "interval time" – that which exists between life and death. Here, Arendt means not only the literal period between the time when a person is born and the moment of their death, but also the reconfiguring of our existence as a rejection of trans-historical economic laws or objectified regulations for managing the subject. Instead, each moment is part of a new effort to make actual that which was once only virtual – to explore the limits of what is possible to discover and find novel ways of experiencing our living reality. In the words of Braun (2007: 20–21):

> Human life here is understood not as a moment in an endlessly racing process whose laws are to be executed on the individual, nor as a manageable entity but as the time span between birth and death. … Politics, finally, would be understood not as the management of populations or the acceleration of economic or scientific progress but as acting in concert together with others, and the purpose of politics would not be to enhance the quality of some collective entity, to create a better species or to maintain the dynamics of the economy, but to make the world a home.

Crucially, Arendt is interested then in the radical domestication of our human existence. She explicitly views politics as an attempt to find ever more alternative modes for "living together". Specifically, Arendt suggests that we use our interval time to find the unique means by which we personally make ourselves "at home" in the world. This implies then a domestication of labour and work to reflect this broader ambitious politics of radical dwelling – its domestication to aid in this freedom to continually make and remake our earthly habitation both personally and in concord with others.

Conclusion

This chapter highlighted Hannah Arendt's profound, continued relevance for organization studies and politics generally. Her reconfiguring of the Marxian concept of alienation, especially, provides a prescient critique for our current neoliberal obsession with management and innovation. Moreover, Arendt points to the fundamental role of organizing as part of the human condition – one with profound political implications. Notably, it is critical that, in our attempts to originally "make ourselves home" in the world, we organize our labour and work to aid this search.

This analysis of course is meant as an introduction and is not exhaustive in its overall analysis. A continuing issue that confronts Arendt is whether her ideas are overly human-centric. Do they have purchase in a world where humans are not the only "intelligent" form of consciousness? Could robots and AI, for instance, one day evolve to be deserving of politics and freedom in the way Arendt describes? As the fourth industrial revolution disrupts our economy, politics and society, it will be interesting to see how Arendtian ideas will continue to inform an emerging "trans-human" condition.

More in the here and now, perhaps, is Arendt's seemingly ignoring of the corporeal dimension of freedom. While she writes at length of the "active life", this is surprisingly devoid of the actual body or embodiment. This gap is especially glaring in light of fresh perspectives that point to how foundational the body must be for any attempts to articulate a radical ethics or politics. Hancock (2008), for example, points to the need for an ethical "generosity" to alternative modes of bodily expression. Within organization studies, Pullen and Rhodes in particular highlight the importance of the corporeal and affective for guiding radical organizational ethics and politics. They note,

> ... ethics in organization manifests politically through resistance that seeks to defy categorization and normalization and the forms of discrimination they invoke. This is a resistance borne out of affective and corporeal encounters with others; encounters marked by generosity and welcome.
>
> (Pullen and Rhodes, 2013: 793)

One way to bridge this gap in the future is to consider Arendt's ideas of critical reflection as a form of "visiting" other ways of being, and as a precursor to a more comprehensive form of "bodily visiting" others' different "homes" in the world.

To conclude, Arendt's ideas continue to hold profound insights for organization studies and organizations generally. She offers a view of providing people with material security, not as an end in itself but as a political beginning. Put differently, she is interested in how individuals can initiate new ways of living and uniquely create a "home" in the world. This politics is one that goes far beyond liberal tolerance, and instead embraces a deeper "generosity" toward others to explore and inaugurate novel forms of existing in the world. Organizations, in turn, should encourage both the economics and politics that foster this radical exploration. Doing so requires that they have the material security to safely make and remake "their home". Arendt thus places an ethical demand that we organize our organizations to allow for individuals to be collectively political. She decries those forms of regulation that undermine this expression of human difference and unprecedented action. Arendt provides the pretext for the study of organizations that do not simply institutionalise the past, but constantly allow for new beginnings. Leaving the last words to Arendt, we affirm that the creation of institutions that remember eternally the "beginning, before it becomes a historical event, is the supreme capacity of man, politically, it is identical with man's freedom" (1968: 479).

Further Readings

Original text by Arendt

Arendt, H. (1961). *Between Past and Future*. New York: Viking Press.

Key academic text

Bloom, P. (2016). *Beyond Power and Resistance: Politics at the Radical Limits*. Lanham, MA: Rowman & Littlefield.

Accessible resource

Young-Bruehl, E. (2009). *Why Arendt Matters*. New Haven, CA: Yale University Press.

References

Allen, A. (2002). Power, subjectivity, and agency: Between Arendt and Foucault. *International Journal of Philosophical Studies*, *10*(2), 131–149.

Arendt, H. (1958). *The Human Condition*. Chicago: The University of Chicago Press.

Arendt, H. (1963). The conquest of space and the stature of man. *The New Atlantis*. https://www.thenewatlantis.com/publications/the-conquest-of-space-and-the-stature-of-man. Accessed on 4 May 2019.

Arendt, H. (1965). *On Revolution*. London: Faber and Faber.

Arendt, H. (1968). *Men in Dark Times*. New York: Harcourt, Brace & Co.

Arendt, H. (1970). *On Violence*. New York: Harvest Books.

Beiner, R. (1990). Hannah Arendt on capitalism and socialism. *Government and Opposition*, *25*(03), 359–370.

Bloom, P. and Rhodes, C. (2018). *The CEO Society: The Corporate Takeover of Everyday Life*. London: Zed.

Braun, K. (2007). Biopolitics and temporality in Arendt and Foucault. *Time & Society*, *16*(1), 5–23.

Breen, K. (2007). Violence and power: A critique of Hannah Arendt on the political. *Philosophy & Social Criticism*, *33*(3), 343–372.

Brown, W. (2015). *Undoing the Demos*. New York: Zone Books.

Canovan, M. (1985). Politics as culture: Hannah Arendt and the public realm. *The History of Political Thought*, 6(3), 617–642.

Canovan, M. (1994). *Hannah Arendt*. Cambridge [UK]: Cambridge University Press.

Cooke, B. (2006). The Cold War origin of action research as managerialist cooptation. *Human Relations*, 59(5), 665–693.

Curthoys, N. (2002). Hannah Arendt and the politics of narrative. *Journal of Narrative Theory*, 32(3), 348–370.

Dean, J. (2016). *Crowds and Party*. New York: Verso Books.

Fleming, P. and Spicer, A. (2004). "You can checkout anytime, but you can never leave": Spatial boundaries in a high commitment organization. *Human Relations*, 57(1), 75–94.

Hancock, P. (2008). Embodied generosity and an ethics of organization. *Organization Studies*, 29(10), 1357–1373.

Herzog, A. (2004). Political itineraries and anarchic cosmopolitanism in the thought of Hannah Arendt. *Inquiry*, 47(1), 20–41.

Honig, B. (1991). Declarations of independence: Arendt and Derrida on the problem of founding a republic. *The American Political Science Review*, 85(1), 97.

Markell, P. (2006). The rule of the people: Arendt, archê, and democracy. *American Political Science Review*, 100(01), 1–14.

Olson, J. (1997). The revolutionary spirit: Hannah Arendt and the anarchists of the Spanish civil war. *Polity*, 29(4), 461–488.

Pullen, A. and Rhodes, C. (2013). Corporeal ethics and the politics of resistance in organizations. *Organization*, 21(6), 782–796.

Spencer, P. (2006). From Rosa Luxemburg to Hannah Arendt: Socialism, barbarism and the extermination camps. *The European Legacy*, 11(5), 527–540.

Vino, A. (1996). Telling stories, reflecting, learning: Hannah Arendt and organization. *Studies in Cultures, Organizations and Societies*, 2(2), 309–325.

Willmott, H. (1993). Strength is ignorance; slavery is freedom: Managing culture in modern organizations. *Journal of Management Studies*, 30(4), 515–552.

7 Decolonising organizations with bell hooks

Helena Liu

> We have all been thrown down so low that nobody thought we'd ever get up again; but we have been long enough trodden now; we will come up again.
>
> —Sojourner Truth

> When intellectual work emerges from a concern with radical social and political change, when that work is directed to the needs of the people, it brings us into greater solidarity and community. It is fundamentally life-enhancing.
>
> —hooks and West (1991, p. 164)

bell hooks[1] is a scholar and social critic whose prolific writings on gender, race and class traverse academic and non-academic arenas. Her formidable body of work comprising 39 books, including five children's books and a book of poetry, boldly challenges what she calls the "imperialist white supremacist capitalist patriarchy" that defines our culture of domination. Written plainly in a way that is accessible to a broad audience, hooks' work names the pain and hurt inflicted by the systemic violence in our society and seek to heal these wounds by inviting possibilities for love. When I read hooks' writings, I am lifted higher. She gives me the vocabulary to speak of my wounds that society bids me to hold silent. Her writings also offer me hope; a shaking urgency to find solidarity with all others who lay trampled beneath imperialist white supremacist capitalist patriarchal power so that we may reclaim and redeem our difference.

hooks' is a defining voice in race studies. Race studies are a moral *tour de force* in countries such as the United States, Canada, the United Kingdom, Australia and New Zealand that seek to confront and reconcile with their brutal histories of slavery and colonialism (Bell, 1995; Bishop, 1998; Chou, 2012; Collins, 2000; Crenshaw, 1991; Delgado and Stefancic, 2012; Ladson-Billings, 1998; Moreton-Robinson, 2000; Pérez

Huber and Solórzano, 2015; Yosso, Smith, Ceja and Solórzano, 2009). Along with intellectual activists in Africa, South America, Asia and the Middle East who give voice to the Global South (Anzaldúa, 1987; Lugones, 2010; Modiri, 2012; Mohanty, 2003; Sankaran and Chng, 2004; Spivak, 2012), scholars who dare speak out against imperialism, white supremacy, capitalism and patriarchy, often do so from the margins of academia and society. Their work has risen against the odds to reveal the fundamental faultlines of coloniality, race, class and gender that undergird social life.

Mainstream research of work and organizations has by and large advanced in isolation from the interdisciplinary developments of race studies. When it is not ignored altogether, race is treated as a fixed, demographic variable in order to measure its effects on the organization. Despite considerable efforts on the part of critical race theorists to challenge essentialist notions of race (Ailon-Souday and Kunda, 2003; Nkomo, 1992), organizational research has for the most part overlooked the invisible dominance of whiteness, while assuming racial difference is measured by traits and behaviours linked to a primordial essence. The socially constructed and politically contested nature of race is suppressed in an act of racism in order to avoid uncomfortable conversations about racism. Even among the self-proclaimed critical voices of management scholars, organizational theorising has demonstrated a certain uneasiness with race, preferring instead to assume whiteness is normal, natural and universal (Liu, 2017c).

hooks' rich, intersectional theorisations of identity and power bring the sterile whiteness of organizational research into sharp relief. While we can now attest to a growing body of literature on gender in management and organizations, we still appear to struggle with understanding the ways gender is cross-cut by sexuality, race, religion, (dis)ability, coloniality, class and other axes of power (Acker, 2012; Cheng, 1999; Collins, 2000, 2012; Holvino, 2010). The dominance of imperialist white feminisms in organization studies has largely silenced alternate voices and in turn reduced inequality and its critique to only the forms that impact elite white women. I hope that through hooks' work, this chapter can interrupt our abiding reduction of identity and power to single-axis issues such as sexism at the expense of any other injustices. It is also my hope that hooks' ideas can help us shift critical and feminist theorising in management and organization studies towards solidarity and united resistance.

In this chapter, I will discuss the ideas that feature throughout hooks' work and highlight their importance to organizational research. The chapter concludes with a reflection on how hooks' philosophy of visionary feminism may valuably shape the future of critical organizational theorising.

A biography of Gloria Jean Watkins

Born Gloria Jean Watkins in 1952, bell hooks grew up with her mother, father and six siblings in the small segregated town of Hopkinsville in rural Kentucky. hooks has frequently reflected on her difficult childhood within her guardedly patriarchal working-class household. They lived in what she would later recall as "an ugly house" where "no one there considered the function of beauty" and so it only "contained a great engulfing emptiness" (hooks, 1990, p. 104). Despite the loneliness she carried, hooks paid tribute to her father's "impressive example of diligence and hard work, approaching tasks with a seriousness of concentration I work to mirror" (hooks, 1989, p. 82), and the ways her mother, like so many Black women, protected their home from the "white supremacist culture of domination" that sought to unmake them as subjects into objects of poverty, hardship and deprivation (hooks, 1990, p. 46).

hooks began her education at the segregated public schools in Kentucky where she encountered passionate African American teachers committed to giving her and the other all-Black pupils a "good education". hooks explained that the education of Black children is not just about preparing them for a vocation, but also about encouraging their engagement with social justice (hooks, 2009b). When the 1960s brought forced school integration to Kentucky, hooks experienced a profound sense of loss. When she arrived at Stanford University on a scholarship, she described being "truly astonished to find teachers who appeared to derive their primary pleasure in the classroom by exercising their authoritarian power over my fellow students, crushing our spirits, and dehumanising our minds and bodies" (hooks, 2009b, p. 2). It was at college that hooks, frustrated by the lack of interest in race issues shown by her white professors, wrote her first major book, *Ain't I a Woman: Black Women and Feminism*, evoking abolitionist Sojourner Truth through the title[2]. hooks was only 19 years old and working as a telephone operator to support herself when she wrote the initial manuscript.

Her pseudonym came from her maternal great-grandmother, "a sharp-tongued woman, a woman who spoke her mind, a woman who was not afraid to talk back" (hooks, 1989, p. 9). By adopting her great-grandmother's name, hooks sought to construct a writer identity that would embrace her spirit as someone who was unafraid to speak out.

When *Ain't I a Woman* was eventually published in 1981 by South End Press, it was harshly criticised by white feminist academics. In deconstructing the racial, heterosexual and class privileges of dominant thinkers at the time, hooks' writings were heretical (Cheng, 1997). However, hooks found that her book was more warmly received by non-academic readers (hooks and West, 1991). To this day, she maintains that her writings need to be accessible to diverse audiences, and eschew academic conventions by using clear, lay language and avoiding references.

Although she had little interest in teaching initially, hooks realised that she could no longer afford to support her writing working long hours in menial jobs. She decided that "teaching was the best profession a writer could have" (hooks, 2009b, p. 3); first lecturing at Santa Cruz, then teaching African American Studies at Yale. In 1988, hooks took a position at Oberlin College in women's studies, where she was able to integrate the discussions of race that were missing from her own undergraduate education. Over time, hooks came to see how she could follow in the steps of progressive teachers and "choose to educate for the practice of freedom" (hooks, 2009b, p. 3). After working in the City College of New York in the 1990s, she returned home to Kentucky and took a position as Distinguished Professor in Residence at Berea College. In 2014, hooks donated her own funds to establish the bell hooks Institute at Berea where she continues to host regular seminars and panels.

Organizing within the imperialist white supremacist capitalist patriarchy

One of the central themes of hooks' work is her use of the term "imperialist white supremacist capitalist patriarchy" to describe the four interlocking systems of power that characterise Euroamerican "dominator culture" (hooks, 2003, 2009a). hooks has not forcefully defined or deconstructed the imperialist white supremacist capitalist patriarchy, and in doing so, appears to encourage a broad understanding and use of her phrase.

hooks has remarked on how her use of this phrase is often met with laughter at her talks and lectures. She does not think naming this system is funny and interprets the laughter of her audience as "a weapon of patriarchal terrorism" that exposes their discomfort in being confronted with feminist disobedience (hooks, 2004, p. 29). Anti-feminist resistance to hooks' provocations notwithstanding, I think that in some cases laughter at the term can come from relief. In hearing someone so openly and calmly delineate the source of the violence in social life generates a kind of lightness. The strangling constriction from a lifetime of biting one's tongue can be released with these five words.

In her writings on imperialism, hooks references the legacies of the Western colonial project that have historically defined exotic "Others" from the epistemic gaze of the West (see also Chakrabarty, 1992; Kwek, 2003; Loomba, 2007; Narayan and Harding, 2000; Prasad, 2003a). Avowing the ascendancy of so-called "objective" Western scientific categorisation (Said, 1978),

European worldviews are then imposed on other cultures and peoples in order to justify and advance European colonialism. Non-white subjects, particularly those in the Global South, are denied their agency for self-definition (Harindranath, 2014; Spivak, 1988). Over time, non-white subjects learned to see themselves through this epistemic gaze, perceiving themselves to be the Other (Liu, 2017a).

This imperialist ideology also lingers in what hooks calls white cultural imperialism. In her essay *Eating the Other*, she describes a white yearning to invade and possess exotic "Others" through appropriation (hooks, 1992). hooks speaks of the ways in which, following the West's own crisis of identity, white cultural producers co-opt Black culture for their own use and, in doing so, displace the voices of Black people and decontextualise their traditions (hooks, 1992). In more recent years, we have seen organizational theorising commit white cultural imperialism via the appropriation of Black feminist theories such as the "outsider within" (Collins, 1986, 1999) and intersectionality (Crenshaw, 1989, 1991). I will return to the white appropriation of Black feminism later in this section.

Contrary to lay uses of "white supremacy" to refer to deviant acts of racial violence, white supremacy as conceptualised within the tradition of race studies refers to the centuries-old racialised social system comprising the "totality of the social relations and practices that reinforce white privilege" (Bonilla-Silva, 2006, p. 9). White supremacy is systemic and operates in and through everyday racism to maintain a strong positive orientation to "white superiority, virtue, moral goodness, and action" (Deitch et al., 2003; Essed, 1991; Feagin, 2013, p. 10; Hill, 2009). It is therefore integral to work and social life (Cheng, 1997; Hunter, Swan, and Grimes, 2010; Liu and Pechenkina, 2016; Parker and Grimes, 2009).

hooks maintains that white supremacy is a more poignant description of race relations in the United States than racism, and indeed, the same could be said of many other white-dominated and postcolonial countries. Both white and non-white people who would not condone outright racial prejudice and violence often continue to support the institution of white supremacy (Bonilla-Silva, 2006; Sullivan, 2014), clenching on to a willful ignorance of the ways white power and privilege define organizational practices. In educated, liberal contexts such as academia, few people would consider themselves racist, yet to varying extents, we remain complicit with Eurocentric knowledge, imperialist pedagogies and research methodologies, while perpetuating prejudicial practices in hiring, promotion and pay (Gillborn, 2005; Leonardo, 2009; Wagner, 2005). The target of hooks' critique is thus not on the actions of a few aberrant individuals – "the racists" – but on the the systemic oppression of racial Otherness under white power and privilege.

The economic system of capitalism is, for hooks, a thoroughly exploitative and dehumanising world order (hooks, 1984, 2000b). Identifying as a democratic socialist, hooks articulates a vision for the redistribution of wealth that will challenge our current class hierarchy (hooks, 2000d). Although hooks (2000d) acknowledges that she has been able to make enough money with her writings to qualify as a member of the upper class, she continues to identify and find solidarity with the poor, working-class community she lived in for the majority of her life. In turn, she is able to exercise her newfound class power in practices of giving that enhance the wellbeing of those more vulnerable (hooks, 2000d). hooks (1990, p. 89), here, engages with a "politics of location", where, within constantly shifting power relations, she rejects the side of the dominator and stands instead in political resistance with the oppressed. For those of us working and teaching in business schools, capitalism can become an all-consuming way of life. Our students are taught to see themselves as commodities to be sold and traded in the labour marketplace. Challenges to capitalist ideologies in our curricula are usually relegated to a peripheral topic on business ethics or corporate social responsibility, lest they threaten our own institutions' capitalistic efforts to sell degrees.

Moderate feminism has promoted for (cis-het, white, elite class, able-bodied) women the importance of acquiring economic and political power, but hooks (1984) argues that it did not offer guidance about the exercise of that power. This oversight allowed capitalism to co-opt feminist visions for change by promoting the illusion that money brings freedom and independence (hooks, 1984). Yet, if the unquestioning accumulation of wealth by women supports the oppression and exploitation of working-class men and women, then it cannot be feminist.

The dismantling of patriarchy as an entrenched system of gender domination is the cornerstone of the visionary feminist movement that hooks represents. Like her preference for the term "white supremacy" rather than "racism" to describe race relations, hooks sees patriarchy as far more descriptive of gender relations in society than sexism per se. In particular, hooks (2009b, p. 170) reminds us that "patriarchy has no gender" and therefore challenges to patriarchy are not reducible to being anti-men.

Men as a group have benefitted and still benefit the most from patriarchy, but the expectation that men should dominate over women within this system takes its toll on the oppressor as well as the oppressed (hooks, 2000b). hooks (1981, p. 114) observes how "patriarchy forces fathers to act as monsters, encourages husbands and lovers to be rapists in disguise; it teaches our blood brothers to feel ashamed that they care for us, and denies all men the emotional life that would act as a humanising, self-affirming force in their lives". When Black people in the United States fought for civil rights, many left assumptions of the imperialist patriarchal system intact. hooks argues that many of the Black men who most vehemently attacked white male power were eager to gain access to that power (hooks, 1981). Their expressions of anger were less a critique of white patriarchal domination than a reaction against their inability to fully participate in that domination (hooks, 1981). At the same time, hooks calls out against the Black women who likewise internalised patriarchal ideologies and expected their Black male partners to financially support them (hooks, 1981).

Although the imperialist white supremacist capitalist patriarchy is rarely cited in organizational theorising, the kindred concept of intersectionality (Crenshaw, 1989, 1991) has risen in popularity among organizational scholars in recent years. Sadly, its application to organizational research has often been misunderstood as a superficial framework for identity categories, for example, supporting a study that looks at "minority ethnic women", yet overlooking power systems of white supremacy and patriarchy that impact their lives (Liu, 2017c). In the collection of ever-more finite combinations of gender, sexuality, race, class, religion, age and language, intersectionality becomes a tool for collating and commodifying difference (Liu, 2017b). Ironically, the Black feminist concept of intersectionality itself has been subject to white cultural imperialism in organizational theorising and research, dislocated from its tradition of racial justice activism (Chun, Lipsitz and Shin, 2013; Collins, 2000; Dhamoon, 2011; Mohanty, 2013; Nash, 2008; The Combahee River Collective, 1977; Yuval-Davis, 2006).

hooks herself rejects the construct of intersectionality and maintains that her theory of the imperialist white supremacist capitalist patriarchy is more informative. Unlike intersectionality, it names the sources of violence in our culture and compels our confrontation with this truth. Despite intersectionality's radical roots, this abstract term in many ways was considered more "palatable" in the imperialist white supremacist capitalist patriarchal academy. Intersectionality's popularity was made possible by its de-politicisation as a happy, unthreatening narrative about diversity (Bilge, 2013; Jibrin and Salem, 2015).

Due to its prevailing positivist and quantitative traditions, organizational research has historically imposed a single-axis view (Tatli and Özbilgin, 2012). Research that treated gender, race and other identity categories as independent variables, and measured their effects on dependent variables such as performance ratings, reinforced the idea that individuals could only experience one injustice at a time: they are subjected to either sexism, racism or some Other *ism*. Positivist and quantitative scholarship has, to date, neglected a richer understanding of context that comprises the dynamic, socially constructed and interlocking nature of identity and power.

The single-axis view has in turn been taken for granted within organizations. The struggle for equality has been largely colonised by elite white women who isolate gender as the only site for change. Blind to their racial, class, heterosexual and able-bodied privileges, they project their values through universal statements that consequently construct all women as victims of male power (hooks, 1981). This reductionistic view ignores the power that elite white women have over non-white, working-class, queer and disabled men, while forcing non-white, working-class, queer and disabled women to align their struggles for equality with elite white women or risk marginalisation and invisibility.

Melinda, a young Asian woman entrepreneur I once interviewed for a study, strained to pinpoint her lived experiences of inequality. She stated, "race hasn't affected me that much; gender sometimes, though I haven't had major issues around sexism ... for me, it's more my age". The way Melinda felt compelled to isolate the most prevalent form of discrimination highlights the constraints of organizational theorising and practice in comprehending the complexity of identity and power. It was also telling that she chose ageism as the site of her struggles. In Australia, frank discussions of sexism and racism still come with considerable professional risk, while age discrimination often appears to be the most apolitical form of injustice and thus the most acceptable to talk about in organizations.

Beyond the confines of management and organizational discourses, concepts such as hooks' imperialist white supremacist capitalist patriarchy offer more powerful frameworks for understanding identity politics in context. In Melinda's case, she would have been allowed to see her embodiment as Asian, cis-female, heterosexual and young-looking as inseparably related to her experiences of inequality. The imperialist and patriarchal representation of young straight Asian females as submissive "lotus blossoms" (Sankaran and Chng, 2004; Tajima, 1989; Zhou and Paul, 2016), combined with white supremacist constructs of the introverted and compliant "model minority" (Chae, 2004; Cho, 1997; Yeh, 2014), meant that Melinda was frequently seen as an "easy target" for bullying. The overarching association of entrepreneurship with white masculinity (Bruni, Gherardi and Poggio, 2004; Knight, 2016; Mirchandani, 1999) within white capitalist patriarchy has meant that Melinda is continually discounted in her field. Her continuous struggles for legitimacy are a product of her subordinated position in the imperialist white supremacist capitalist patriarchal hierarchy.

For us scholars, hooks' writings show a way to write that acknowledges our own implication in knowledge production. Her approach rejects the positivistic imagining of the researcher as separate from the researched; a disembodied voice of authority who impassively determines how to categorise the social world. Always remaining aware of our locations in the imperialist white supremacist capitalist patriarchy impels us to question our own complicity within these systems of power. With language also a site of struggle, writing differently in our scholarship – writing emotionally, reflexively, using the vernacular of the oppressed (hooks, 1990) – has the potential to decolonise organizational theorising as well as the academy.

Finding hooks' visionary feminism

Throughout her work, hooks distinguishes the various agendas of moderate, white and bourgeois feminisms from one that carries an enduring commitment to dismantle the imperialist white supremacist capitalist patriarchy. hooks calls her praxis a visionary feminism. In her essay *To Love Again*, hooks (2000c, p. 103) declares that visionary feminism is "a wise and loving politic. The soul of our politics is the commitment to ending domination. Love can never take root in a relationship based on domination and coercion".

However, hooks warns that when it is in the interests of the imperialist white supremacist capitalist patriarchy to suppress revolutionary politics, visionary feminism is constantly at risk of being deradicalised. Confining political change to one axis of power at a time preserves the dominator culture as a whole. For hooks, white men are willing to consider women's rights when the granting of those rights could serve the interests of maintaining white supremacy (hooks, 2000b). As the (predominantly elite white) women began to gain economic power in the existing social structure, they let go of their commitment to a revolutionary politics that would threaten that social structure (hooks, 2000b).

hooks notes that while visionary feminist thinking is perhaps most accepted and embraced in academic circles, it has become increasingly produced through exclusionary language comprehensible only by people who are highly literate, well-educated, and, more often than not, materially privileged. Hooks urges feminist scholars to reject academic careerism and re-engage with a radical politics that reaches a broader audience. Visionary feminism has the potential to be grassroots and community-based, with the power to speak to practitioners as well as scholars. Corporate professionals who are deepest within the belly of the imperialist white supremacist capitalist patriarchy are rarely thrown the lifeline of visionary feminism. They are left instead to contend with the likes of *Lean In*, *#GIRLBOSS* and *The Confidence Code* – reductionistic, accessible texts that promote a neoliberal fantasy of gender parity while leaving imperialist white supremacist capitalist, and even patriarchal, practices intact. Although there have been compelling calls towards a visionary feminist agenda that directs our intellectualism towards dismantling the imperialist white supremacist capitalist patriarchy (Acker, 2012; Grimes, 2001; Holvino, 2010; Nkomo, 1992; Prasad, 2003b), these attempts have to date largely remained on the periphery of organization studies. Revolutionary change, for the most part, remains unspeakable in our field.

It is perhaps more necessary than ever that, as critical scholars working in management and organizations, we release ourselves from the stranglehold of imperialism, white supremacy, capitalism and patriarchy in the academy. As hooks has shown us, we self-declared feminists, socialists, anti-racists and anti-colonialists cannot win our fights along a single axis. We need to learn to build solidarity with those who may not share our oppressions and resist all the interlocking forms of domination in our society (hooks, 1984).

Just as the eradication of patriarchy liberates women, men and all those who identify otherwise, the dismantling of white supremacy has the potential to liberate all of us, regardless if we identify as white or non-white. White female organizational scholars who have critiqued the gender blindness of their male counterparts can similarly overlook issues of race in their own theorising. hooks (1984) observes that whiteness among women is often an invisible bond, a racial identity wholly based on the experience of non-white people as the Other and as a threat. Although many white feminists will insist on a shared sense of womanhood, this affirmation belies the way they noticeably become tense when a woman of colour enters the room (hooks, 1984; Moraga and Anzaldúa, 1983). As long as white feminists deny and uphold white supremacy, there can be no solidarity between them and women of colour in the vital challenge against patriarchy.

The answer, for hooks, is to make love the foundation of our visionary feminist politics. Love, in dominator culture, has been manipulated into a form of control. In heteropatriarchal bonds, it was assumed that women, being the nurturing, caring partner, would give love, while powerful men in return would provide and protect (hooks, 2000c). Likewise, in white societies, the colonised Others are expected to adore and admire their more civilised colonisers who believed they were bringing the rest of the world into modernity. Visionary feminism helps us love beyond the bonds of domination (hooks, 2000a). That love must be "rooted in recognition and acceptance, that love combines acknowledgment, care, responsibility, commitment, and knowledge" (hooks, 2000c, p. 104). The visionary feminist's turn towards love in organizations has been poignantly theorised by Vachhani (2015), for whom writing is a powerful feminist tool (see also Steyaert, 2015). Feminist writing has the potential to reconstruct how the feminine is co-opted in the service of organizations and to reclaim organizational spaces with the voices of gendered, racialised, classed and aged subjects who have been traditionally marginalised. As hooks has done, Vachhani (2015) rallies visionary feminists to resist confining our writing to theoretically impenetrable expressions enclaved within academic journals and, instead, to activate our writing by disseminating it more widely.

bell hooks is a consummate visionary feminist. Her work is firmly grounded in the concrete constraints of our present reality, while simultaneously imagining the possibilities beyond that reality. Her work speaks to academics and non-academics alike, of all classes, genders and racial identifications. hooks' writings reach out to all of us who have been dehumanised within the dominator culture. As so many organizations institutionalise the imperialist white supremacist capitalist patriarchy, work itself can often be dehumanising. By following in hooks' steadfast intellectual integrity and emotional honesty (Cheng, 1997), we may cultivate a visionary feminist intellectualism that names the violence inflicted by organizations and creates the space for us to find redemption, healing and love.

Notes

1 bell hooks' name is not capitalised throughout the chapter following her desire to place the focus on her ideas rather than herself.
2 Sojourner Truth delivered her speech, "Ain't I a Woman?" in 1851 at the Women's Rights Convention in Akron, Ohio. The context and various transcriptions of the speech can be found at http://sojournertruthmemorial.org/sojourner-truth/her-words/.

Further Reading

Original text by hooks

hooks, b. (1984). *Feminist Theory: From Margin to Center*. Boston, MA: South End.

Key academic text

del Guadalupe Davidson, M. and Yancy, G. (Eds.). (2009). *Critical Perspectives on bell hooks*. New York, NY: Routledge.

Accessible resource

Video of bell hooks and Laverne Cox's Public Dialogue at The New School: https://www.youtube.com/watch?v=9oMmZIJijgY. bell hooks was scholar-in-residence at Eugene Lang College at The New School for Liberal Arts (https://www.newschool.edu/lang) between 2013 and 2015, and a series of her recorded panels and dialogues are available on The New School YouTube Channel.

References

Acker, J. (2012). Theorizing gender, race, and class in organizations. In E. Jeanes, D. Knights and P. Yancey Martin (Eds.), *Handbook of Gender, Work and Organization* (pp. 65–80). Chicester: Wiley.

Ailon-Souday, G. and Kunda, G. (2003). The local selves of global workers: The social construction of national identity in the face of organizational globalization. *Organization Studies*, *24*(7), 1073–1096.

Anzaldúa, G. E. (1987). *Borderlands/La Frontera: The New Mestiza*. San Francisco, CA: Aunt Lute Books.

Bell, D. A. (1995). Who's afraid of critical race theory? *University of Illinois Law Review*, *1995*, 893–910.

Bilge, S. (2013). Intersectionality undone: Saving intersectionality from feminist intersectionality studies. *Du Bois Review*, *10*(2), 405–424.

Bishop, R. (1998). Freeing ourselves from neo-colonial domination in research: A Maori approach to creating knowledge. *International Journal of Qualitative Studies in Education*, *11*(2), 199–219.

Bonilla-Silva, E. (2006). *Racism without Racists: Color-Blind Racism and the Persistence of Racial Inequality in the United States*. Lanham, MA: Rowman & Littlefield Publishers.

Bruni, A., Gherardi, S. and Poggio, B. (2004). Doing gender, doing entrepreneurship: An ethnographic account of intertwined practices. *Gender, Work and Organization*, *11*(4), 406–429.

Chae, H. S. (2004). Talking back to the Asian model minority discourse: Korean-origin youth experiences in high school. *Journal of Intercultural Studies*, *25*(1), 59–73.

Chakrabarty, D. (1992). Postcoloniality and the artifice of history: Who speaks for "Indian" pasts? *Representations*, *1*(37), 1–26.

Cheng, C. (1997). A review essay on the books of bell hooks: Organizational diversity lessons from a thoughtful race and gender heretic. *Academy of Management Review*, *22*(2), 553–574.

Cheng, C. (1999). Marginalized masculinities and hegemonic masculinity: An introduction. *The Journal of Men's Studies*, *7*(3), 295–315.

Cho, S. K. (1997). Converging stereotypes in racialized sexual harassment: Where the model minority meets Suzie Wong. *Journal of Gender, Race and Justice*, *1*(1), 177–211.

Chou, R. S. (2012). *Asian American Sexual Politics: The Construction of Race, Gender, and Sexuality*. Lanham, MA: Rowman & Littlefield Publishers.

Chun, J. J., Lipsitz, G. and Shin, Y. (2013). Intersectionality as a social movement strategy: Asian immigrant women advocates. *Signs: Journal of Women in Culture and Society*, *38*(4), 917–940.

Collins, P. H. (1986). Learning from the outsider within: The sociological significance of black feminist thought. *Social Problems*, *33*(6), S14–S32.

Collins, P. H. (1999). Reflections on the outsider within. *Journal of Career Development*, *26*(1), 85–88.

Collins, P. H. (2000). *Black Feminist Thought: Knowledge, Consciousness, and the Politics of Empowerment*, (2nd ed.). Hoboken, NJ: Taylor & Francis.

Collins, P. H. (2012). Social inequality, power, and politics: Intersectionality and American pragmatism in dialogue. *Journal of Speculative Philosophy, 26*(2), 442–457.

Crenshaw, K. (1989). Demarginalizing the intersection of race and sex: A black feminist critique of antidiscrimination doctrine, feminist theory, and antiracist politics. *University of Chicago Legal Forum, 1989*(1), 139–167.

Crenshaw, K. (1991). Mapping the margins: Intersectionality, identity politics, and violence against women of color. *Stanford Law Review, 43*(6), 1241–1299.

Deitch, E. A., Barsky, A., Butz, R. M., Chan, S., Brief, A. P. and Bradley, J. (2003). Subtle yet significant: The existence and impact of everyday racial discrimination in the workplace. *Human Relations, 56*(11), 1299–1324.

Delgado, R. and Stefancic, J. (Eds.). (2012). *Critical Race Theory: An Introduction*, (2nd ed.). New York: New York University Press.

Dhamoon, R. K. (2011). Considerations on mainstreaming intersectionality. *Political Research Quarterly, 64*(1), 230–243.

Essed, P. (1991). *Understanding Everyday Racism: An Interdisciplinary Theory*. Newbury Park, CA: Sage.

Feagin, J. R. (2013). *The White Racial Frame: Centuries of Racial Framing and Counter-Framing*. New York, NY: Routledge.

Gillborn, D. (2005). Education policy as an act of white supremacy: Whiteness, critical race theory and education reform. *Journal of Education Policy, 20*(4), 485–505.

Grimes, D. S. (2001). Putting our own house in order: Whiteness, change and organization studies. *Journal of Organizational Change Management, 14*(2), 132–149.

Harindranath, R. (2014). The view from the Global South: An introduction. *Postcolonial Studies, 17*(2), 109–114.

Hill, J. H. (2009). *The Everyday Language of White Racism*. Chichester: John Wiley & Sons.

Holvino, E. (2010). Intersections: The simultaneity of race, gender and class in organization studies. *Gender, Work and Organization, 17*(3), 248–277.

hooks, b. (1981). *Ain't I a Woman: Black Women and Feminism*. Boston: South End.

hooks, b. (1984). *Feminist Theory: From Margin to Center*. Boston, MA: South End.

hooks, b. (1989). *Talking Back: Thinking Feminist, Thinking Black*. Boston: South End.

hooks, b. (1990). *Yearning: Race, Gender, and Cultural Politics*. Boston: South End.

hooks, b. (1992). Eating the other. In b. hooks, *Black Looks: Race and Representation* (pp. 21–39). Boston: South End Press.

hooks, b. (2000a). *All About Love: New Visions*. New York: William Morrow and Company.

hooks, b. (2000b). *Feminism Is for Everybody: Passionate Politics*. London: Pluto Press.

hooks, b. (2000c). To love again: The heart of feminism. In *Feminism Is for Everybody: Passionate Politics* (pp. 100–104). London: Pluto Press.

hooks, b. (2000d). *Where We Stand: Class Matters*. London: Routledge.

hooks, b. (2003). *We Real Cool: Black Men and Masculinity*. Hoboken, NJ: Taylor and Francis.

hooks, b. (2004). *The Will to Change: Men, Masculinity, and Love*. New York, NY: Atria Books.

hooks, b. (2009a). *Belonging: A Culture of Place*. New York, NY: Routledge.

hooks, b. (2009b). *Teaching Critical Thinking: Practical Wisdom*. Hoboken, NJ: Taylor and Francis.

hooks, b. and West, C. (1991). *Breaking Bread: Insurgent Black Intellectual Life*. Boston, MA: South End Press.

Hunter, S., Swan, E. and Grimes, D. S. (2010). Introduction: Reproducing and resisting whiteness in organizations, policies, and places. *Social Politics, 17*(4), 407–422.

Jibrin, R. and Salem, S. (2015). Revisiting intersectionality: Reflections on theory and praxis. *Trans-Scripts, 5*, 7–24.

Knight, M. (2016). Race-ing, classing and gendering racialized women's participation in entrepreneurship. *Gender, Work & Organization, 23*(3), 310–327.

Kwek, D. (2003). Decolonizing and re-presenting culture's consequences: A postcolonial critique of cross-cultural studies in management. In A. Prasad (Ed.), *Postcolonial Theory and Organizational Analysis: A Critical Engagement* (pp. 121–146). New York: Palgrave Macmillan.

Ladson-Billings, G. (1998). Just what is critical race theory and what's it doing in a nice field like education? *Qualitative Studies in Education, 11*(1), 7–24.

Leonardo, Z. (2009). *Race, whiteness, and Education*. New York, NY: Routledge.

Liu, H. (2017a). Beneath the white gaze: Strategic self-orientalism among Chinese Australians. *Human Relations, 70*(7), 781–804.

Liu, H. (2017b). Just the servant: An intersectional critique of servant leadership. *Journal of Business Ethics*, 1–14. doi:10.1007/s10551-017-3633-0.

Liu, H. (2017c). Redeeming difference in CMS through anti-racist feminisms. In A. Pullen, N. Harding and M. Phillips (Eds.), *Feminists and Queer Theorists Debate the Future of Critical Management Studies* (Vol. 3, pp. 39–56). Bingley: Emerald Group.

Liu, H. and Pechenkina, E. (2016). Staying quiet or rocking the boat? An autoethnography of organisational visual white supremacy. *Equality, Diversity and Inclusion: An International Journal, 35*(3), 186–204.

Loomba, A. (2007). *Colonialism/Postcolonialism*, (2nd ed.). Milton Park: Routledge.

Lugones, M. (2010). Toward a decolonial feminism. *Hypatia, 25*(4), 742–759.

Mirchandani, K. (1999). Feminist insight on gendered work: New directions in research on women and entrepreneurship. *Gender, Work & Organization, 6*(4), 224–235.

Modiri, J. M. (2012). The colour of law, power and knowledge: Introducing critical race theory in (post-) apartheid South Africa. *South African Journal on Human Rights, 28*(3), 405–436.

Mohanty, C. T. (2003). *Feminism without Borders: Decolonizing Theory, Practicing Solidarity*, (2nd ed.). Durham: Duke University Press.

Mohanty, C. T. (2013). Transnational feminist crossings: On neoliberalism and radical critique. *Signs: Journal of Women in Culture and Society, 38*(4), 967–991.

Moraga, C. and Anzaldúa, G. E. (Eds.). (1983). *This Bridge Called My Back: Writings by Radical Women of Color*, (2nd ed.). New York: Kitchen Table: Women of Color Press.

Moreton-Robinson, A. (2000). Troubling business: Difference and whiteness within feminism. *Australian Feminist Studies*, *15*(33), 343–352.

Narayan, U. and Harding, S. G. (2000). *Decentering the Center: Philosophy for a Multicultural, Postcolonial, and Feminist World*. Bloomington, IN: Indiana University Press.

Nash, J. C. (2008). Re-thinking intersectionality. *Feminist Review*, *89*(1), 1–15.

Nkomo, S. M. (1992). The emperor has no clothes: Rewriting "race in organizations". *The Academy of Management Review*, *17*(3), 487–513.

Parker, P. S. and Grimes, D. S. (2009). "Race" and management communication. In F. Bargiela-Chiappini (Ed.), *The Handbook of Business Discourse* (pp. 292–304). Edinburgh: Edinburgh University Press.

Pérez Huber, L. and Solórzano, D. G. (2015). Visualizing everyday racism: Critical race theory, visual microaggressions, and the historical image of Mexican banditry. *Qualitative Inquiry*, *21*(3), 223–238.

Prasad, A. (Ed.). (2003a). *Postcolonial Theory and Organizational Analysis: A Critical Engagement*. New York: Palgrave Macmillan.

Prasad, A. (2003b). The gaze of the other: Postcolonial theory and organizational analysis. In A. Prasad (Ed.), *Postcolonial Theory and Organizational Analysis: A Critical Engagement* (pp. 3–43). New York: Palgrave Macmillan.

Said, E. W. (1978). *Orientalism*. London: Penguin.

Sankaran, C. and Chng, H. H. (2004). "We women aren't free to die": Transacting Asian sexualities in a feminism classroom in Singapore. *Critical Asian Studies*, *36*(2), 285–301.

Spivak, G. C. (1988). Can the subaltern speak? In C. Nelson and L. Grossberg (Eds.), *Marxism and the Interpretation of Culture* (pp. 271–313). Basingstoke: Macmillian Education.

Spivak, G. C. (2012). Subaltern studies: Deconstructing historiography. In G. C. Spivak, *In other Worlds: Essays in Cultural Politics* (pp. 270–304). Hoboken, NJ: Taylor and Francis.

Steyaert, C. (2015). Three women. A kiss. A life. On the queer writing of time in organization. *Gender, Work and Organization*, *22*(2), 163–178.

Sullivan, S. (2014). *Good White People: The Problem with Middle-Class White Anti-Racism*. Albany, NY: SUNY.

Tajima, R. E. (1989). Lotus blossoms don't bleed: Images of Asian women. In Asian Women United (Ed.), *Making Waves: An Anthology of Writings by and about Asian American Women* (pp. 308–317). Boston: Beacon Press.

Tatli, A. and Özbilgin, M. F. (2012). An emic approach to intersectional study of diversity at work: A Bourdieuan framing. *International Journal of Management Reviews*, *14*(2), 180–200.

The Combahee River Collective. (1977). A black feminist statement. In T. P. McCarthy and J. McMillian (Eds.), *Protest Nation: Words That Inspired a Century of American Radicalism* (pp. 212–216). New York: The New Press.

Vachhani, S. (2015). Organizing love–Thoughts on the transformative and activist potential of feminine writing. *Gender, Work and Organization, 22*(2), 148–162.

Wagner, A. E. (2005). Unsettling the academy: Working through the challenges of anti-racist pedagogy. *Race Ethnicity and Education, 8*(3), 261–275.

Yeh, D. (2014). Contesting the "model minority": Racialization, youth culture and "British Chinese"/"Oriental" nights. *Ethnic and Racial Studies, 37*(7), 1197–1210.

Yosso, T. J., Smith, W., Ceja, M. and Solórzano, D. G. (2009). Critical race theory, racial microaggressions, and campus racial climate for Latina/o undergraduates. *Harvard Educational Review, 79*(4), 659–690.

Yuval-Davis, N. (2006). Intersectionality and feminist politics. *European Journal of Women's Studies, 13*(3), 193–209.

Zhou, Y. and Paul, B. (2016). Lotus Blossom or Dragon Lady: A content analysis of "Asian women" online pornography. *Sexuality & Culture, 20*(4), 1083–1100.

Index

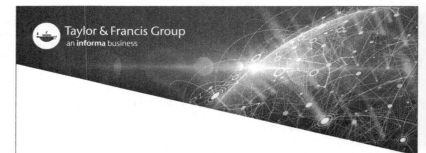

Printed in the United States
by Baker & Taylor Publisher Services